MONDAY MORNING QUARTERBACKS, HERE'S YOUR GAME!

1) Who was the first Super Bowl MVP who was *not* a quarterback?
2) Which NFL player was in the movie M*A*S*H?
3) True or False. Red Miller took the Denver Broncos to Super Bowl XII in his first year as head coach of the team.

If you thought you knew the answers to these questions but didn't, *or* if these were a snap, but you want more fascinating (and sometimes bizarre) teasers and tidbits about your favorite sport,

THE SUPER OFFICIAL
NFL TRIVIA BOOK

is your super source of significant fun!

Answers: 1) Chuck Howley, Dallas linebacker
2) Ben Davidson
3) True

Join the NFL's Newest Team:
The NFL SuperPro Club

Kids, here's a great new way to have football fun—become a member of the NFL SuperPro Club. For only $7.00 you get all this in two big mailings:

1984/85 Team Calendar

Official Membership Card customized with your favorite team's logo.

Team Posterbook

Official NFL SuperPro Club Newsletters

Player Photos/Team Fact Sheet

NFL Team Decal

Official Membership Certificate signed by NFL Commissioner Pete Rozelle.

NFL Standings Board

Joining the NFL SuperPro Club is easy. Just fill out the coupon below and send it with a check or money order for $7.00* (no cash please) to: NFL SuperPro Club, P.O. Box 8888, Trenton, N.J. 08650.

_____ _____

Name   Age

_____

Address

_____

City   State   Zip

_____ _____

Telephone   Favorite NFL team

* Foreign memberships are $12. Membership kits will be mailed beginning September 1, 1984. Please allow 4-6 weeks for delivery.

THE SUPER OFFICIAL

NFL TRIVIA BOOK

Ted Brock and Jim Campbell

All contents are accurate as of February 15, 1985

A SIGNET BOOK

NEW AMERICAN LIBRARY

PHOTO CREDITS

(The numbers following names are the Photo Trivia question numbers in
The Second Official NFL Trivia Book.)

Fred Anderson 27; Alex Barkoff 23; John Biever 31; Vernon Biever 16, 36;
David Boss 1, 12; Buffalo Bills 17; Brown University 13; Columbia
Pictures 28; Malcolm Emmons 14; Nate Fine 33; Russell Kriwanek 35;
University of Michigan 8c; Minnesota Vikings 24; New Orleans Saints 22;
University of Notre Dame 30; Sal Portero 7; Pro Football Hall of Fame 3,
8a 8b, 10, 15, 19, 20, 21, 25; Frank Rippon 32; Ron Ross 29;
Manny Rubio 2; Barry Staver 34; Vic Stein 18; Corky Trewin 9; Universal
Pictures 11; Herb Weitman 6; Wide World Photos 26; Lou Witt 4;
Yale University 5.

The First Official NFL Trivia Book and *The Second Official NFL Trivia Book*
were originally published as separate volumes by New American Library.

THE FIRST OFFICIAL
NFL TRIVIA BOOK

Ted Brock and Jim Campbell

All contents are accurate as of February 15, 1985

Contents

NFL Trivia Quiz

Unless we miss our guess, your chances of a perfect score on the 150 questions that follow are razor-thin. But that's to be expected from an exercise as trivial as this one. You'll notice, along the way, that we've thrown in some random tidbits culled from the NFL's history. Think of them as "breathers" if you like . . . when you're dealing with microscopic information, it helps to give your eyes a rest, a "freebie" if you will, every now and then. Answers to the quiz begin on page 165.

1. Side by Side

Which two NFL running backs played in the same college backfield?

   a. O.J. Simpson and Ricky Bell
   b. Tony Dorsett and Otis Armstrong
   c. Sherman Smith and Earl Campbell
   d. Franco Harris and Lydell Mitchell
   e. Walter Payton and Roland Harper
   f. Rob Lytle and Rob Carpenter

2. Running against the grain

Identify the running back whose number was/is NOT 32:

   a. Jim Brown
   b. Gale Sayers
   c. Franco Harris
   d. O.J. Simpson
   e. Ottis Anderson
   f. Marcus Allen

3. Also-rans?

John Riggins holds the NFL record for scoring 24 touchdowns in a season. Identify the running back who is in second place with 23.

   a. Franco Harris
   b. Sam Cunningham
   c. Dick Bass
   d. Jim Brown
   e. O.J. Simpson
   f. Pete Banaszak

4. Now batting for WHOM?

Which former 49ers running back was the only man ever to pinch-hit for the legendary Ted Williams?

    a. Hugh McElhenny
    b. Carroll Hardy
    c. Jim Brown
    d. Chuck Essegian
    e. Y.A. Tittle
    f. Vic Janowicz

When it comes to the first "overall" draft choice each year, the player chosen has usually been a glamour-position type. A quarterback, a running back, and more recently a defensive player—a lineman or linebacker. Only once since the combined draft of 1967 was an offensive lineman taken. The Minnesota Vikings took tackle Ron Yary of USC as the very first choice in 1968. Yary rewarded their confidence with 15 all-pro caliber seasons. He played a final year with the Rams in 1982.

5. Good stock

Which former member of the Atlanta Falcons is the son of a Samoan chieftain?

   a. Rolland Lawrence
   b. Wilson Faumuina
   c. Steve Bartkowski
   d. Garth Ten Napel
   e. Fulton Kuykendall
   f. Lou Kirouae

6. Goal-oriented

Who holds the NFL record for scoring in the most consecutive games (151)?

   a. George Blanda
   b. Fred Cox
   c. Gino Cappelletti
   d. Gale Sayers
   e. Walter Payton
   f. Lenny Moore

Third-year offensive tackle Luis Sharpe of the St. Louis Cardinals was born in Havanna, Cuba, in 1960. However, he attended high school in Detroit and college at UCLA.

7. Man for two seasons

Who is the only man to manage a major league baseball team and coach an NFL football team?

- a. Casey Stengel
- b. Charlie Dressen
- c. Hugo Bezdek
- d. Dan Jesse
- e. Frank Leahy
- f. Clark Shaughnessy

8. Penetrate this one

Complete the famous front-four combinations.

a. Rams: Lamar Lundy, Rosey Grier, Deacon Jones, and _____.

b. Vikings: Jim Marshall, Gary Larsen, Carl Eller, and _____.

c. Steelers: L.C. Greenwood, Dwight White, Ernie Holmes, and _____.

d. Dolphins: Vern Den Herder, Bob Heinz, Bill Stanfill, and _____.

e. Cowboys: Harvey Martin, Larry Cole, Randy White and _____.

9. Welcome

True or false? The Pro Football Hall of Fame's class of 1984 includes Mike McCormack, Charley Taylor, Arnie Weinmeister, and Willie Wood.

10. Precocious

Name the two members of the Pro Football Hall of Fame who played only junior college football before playing in the NFL.

11. The whole enchilada

Which man played more seasons, more games, and scored more points than anyone in NFL history?

- a. Jim Brown
- b. Fran Tarkenton
- c. Jim Marshall
- d. Jim Turner
- e. Johnny Unitas
- f. George Blanda

12. Clockwork

Jim Marshall, the 42-year-old Minnesota Vikings defensive end, retired at the end of the 1979 season with the NFL record for consecutive games played. How many?

- a. 1,230
- b. 150
- c. 282
- d. 521
- e. 88
- f. 310

13. Idles of March

Which NFL player was NOT an outstanding track athlete as well?

   a. Curley Culp
   b. Clifford Branch
   c. Mel Gray
   d. Bob Hayes
   e. O.J. Simpson
   f. Renaldo (Skeets) Nehemiah

14. Triple threat

Name the man who played halfback in the NFL, umpired major league baseball, and coached professional basketball.

   a. Clarence Peaks
   b. Volney Quinlan
   c. Larry Brown
   d. Hank Soar
   e. Burl Toler
   f. Jim Tunney

Pro Football Hall of Fame member Bobby Layne and three-time All-American Doak Walker played together in the Detroit Lions' backfield for six years in the 1950s. Layne and Walker had played quarterback and halfback together at Highland Park High School in Dallas.

15. Breaking the barrier

In 1984 which runner joined Walter Payton, Jim Brown, Franco Harris, and O.J. Simpson as the only players to pass 10,000 yards rushing in an NFL career?

a. Eric Dickerson
b. Tony Dorsett
c. John Riggins
d. Earl Campbell
e. William Andrews
f. Billy Sims

16. But can he dunk?

Which NFL wide receiver is a son-in-law of the famous basketball dribbling wizard, Marques Haynes?

a. Cliff Branch, Raiders
b. Drew Pearson, Cowboys
c. Louis Lipps, Steelers
d. Alfred Jackson, Falcons
e. James Lofton, Packers
f. Guido Merkens, Saints

On a two-game trip to Japan and Hawaii in 1976, the San Diego Chargers got in two workouts in one day. Unusual? Not until you consider that the two sessions were 3,700 miles apart. After training in Tokyo on a Thursday morning, the team caught a 7:30 p.m. flight, crossed the international date line, and reached Honolulu at 6:30 a.m. the same day, just in time for a few hours' sleep and another workout that afternoon.

17. Undergraduate work

Which present-day NFL running back holds the NCAA rushing record with 6,082 yards in a four-year college career?

    a. Billy Sims, Lions
    b. Earnest Jackson, Chargers
    c. Eric Dickerson, Rams
    d. Tony Dorsett, Cowboys
    e. Earl Campbell, Saints
    f. Walter Payton, Bears

18. Signed and delivered

Who was the first player chosen in the NFL's first draft in 1936 to actually play in the NFL?

  a. Sammy Baugh
  b. Riley Smith
  c. Don Hutson
  d. Jay Berwanger
  e. Dan Fortmann
  f. Armand Niccolai

19. It exists, he exists

Name the former all-pro performer from Ouachita Baptist University.

  a. Cliff Harris, Cowboys
  b. Carlos Pennywell, Patriots
  c. Lynn Swann, Steelers
  d. Pat Thomas, Rams
  e. Willie Alexander, Oilers
  f. Ken Houston, Redskins

20. He had to start somewhere

Which American novelist began his writing career as a cub reporter covering an NFL team—the Pottsville (Pennsylvania) Maroons—in the 1920s?

a. John O'Hara
b. Ernest Hemingway
c. F. Scott Fitzgerald
d. James Jones
e. Norman Mailer
f. John Updike

21. Heady topic

What is unique about the Cleveland Browns' helmet?

a. The Browns are the only team that still uses leather helmets.
b. The helmets glow in the dark.
c. They are equipped with citizens band radios.
d. They cost $500 each.
e. The Browns are the only NFL team not displaying a logo.
f. The Browns are the only NFL team to have "home" and "away" helmets.

22. Airborne

Which NFL receiver teamed with Y.A. Tittle to introduce the "Alley Oop" pass?

a. Frank Gifford
b. R.C. Owens
c. Clyde Connor
d. Bobby Walston
e. Billy Howton
f. Billy Wilson

23. New baby

By what name was the National Football League known during its first two seasons, 1920 and 1921?

a. United Football League
b. American Football League
c. American Professional Football Association
d. National Professional Football League
e. All-America Football Conference
f. Continental Football League

24. Pioneers

The Green Bay Packers' franchise is unique for two reasons. One is that it represents the NFL's smallest city. What is the other?

a. It is the oldest franchise in the league.
b. It is community-owned.
c. It has never won a championship.
d. Its stadium is the only one in the league without lights.
e. It began play as part of the United Football League.
f. All its head coaches have been ex-Packers players.

In the 1965 playoff for the Western Division championship of the NFL, Baltimore's Tom Matte played the entire game at quarterback with the Colts' game plan taped to his wrist. Starter Johnny Unitas and backup Gary Cuozzo both were injured, and Matte, a running back who had played quarterback at Ohio State, got the call—and the NFL's first portable "crib sheet." The Colts lost to Green Bay 13–10 in sudden death overtime.

25. "You can call me . . ."

Match the player from the first column with his given name in the second column.

1. Red Grange		a.	Richard
2. Sonny Jurgensen		b.	Christian
3. Night Train Lane		c.	Frank
4. Crazylegs Hirsch		d.	John
5. Red Badgro		e.	Wilbur
6. Dutch Clark		f.	Earl
7. Paddy Driscoll		g.	David
8. Weeb Ewbank		h.	Elroy
9. Deacon Jones		i.	Harold
10. Bruiser Kinard		j.	Morris

26. Around the clock

Called "The Last of the 60-Minute Men," this Pro Football Hall of Famer played nearly the entire game in a series of crucial victories as his team drove for the 1960 NFL title. Who is he?

a. Chuck Bednarik, Eagles
b. Sam Huff, Giants
c. Bill George, Bears
d. Ray Nitschke, Packers
e. Dave Wilcox, 49ers
f. Joe Schmidt, Lions

The first NFL championship played indoors was not *Super Bowl XII in the New Orleans Superdome. It was the 1932 meeting between the Portsmouth Spartans and the Chicago Bears, held at Chicago Stadium, a hockey rink that afforded an 80-yard field covered with dirt left over from a recent circus. The Bears beat the Spartans 9–0, scoring their touchdown on a pass from Bronko Nagurski to Red Grange and later adding a safety.*

27. On the rebound

Name the NFL coach who delayed his NFL playing career two years to play with the Minneapolis Lakers of the NBA.

   a. Tom Landry, Cowboys
   b. Bud Grant, Vikings
   c. Bill Walsh, 49ers
   d. Marion Campbell, Eagles
   e. Don Cornell, Chargers
   f. Joe Gibbs, Redskins

28. Hint: They're not cousins

What do the following have in common?
    Don Horn
    Dennis Shaw
    Brian Sipe
    Bill Donckers
    Jesse Freitas

29. Busy man

Name the pro halfback who gained 1,432 yards rushing and 1,442 yards passing in a single season.

    a. Bobby Douglass, Chicago Bears, 1968
    b. Orban (Spec) Sanders, New York Yankees (AAFC), 1947
    c. Beattie Feathers, Chicago Bears, 1934
    d. Roger Staubach, Dallas Cowboys, 1976
    e. Norm Van Brocklin, Philadelphia Eagles, 1957
    f. Buddy Young, Brooklyn Dodgers (AAFC), 1949

30. Good resume

Although he did not play college football, he was a successful high school head coach, college assistant and head coach, and a pro assistant before being elevated to the head coaching job of the Detroit Lions in the 1970s. Who is he?

   a. Joe Schmidt
   b. Tommy Hudspeth
   c. Rick Forzano
   d. Lou Holtz
   e. Harry Gilmer
   f. Bud Grant

31. He lived for fourth down

Which NFL player holds the record for the most career punts, 1,072?

   a. Norm Van Brocklin
   b. Pat Brady
   c. John James
   d. Jerrel Wilson
   e. Bobby Walden
   f. Sammy Baugh

32. His weekly bread basket

Going into the 1984 season Harold Carmichael held the NFL record for consecutive games with at least one reception. How many games?

a. 105
b. 107
c. 216
d. 83
e. 127
f. 288

33. Standing on ceremony

Name the only man who has been enshrined in the Pro Football Hall of Fame, the College Football Hall of Fame, and the Baseball Hall of Fame.

a. Hank Soar
b. George Halas
c. Cal Hubbard
d. Casey Stengel
e. Joe McCarthy
f. Hank Sauer

34. Roll Tide roll

Pro Football Hall of Famer Don Hutson of the Green Bay Packers was one end on Alabama's 1935 Rose Bowl champions. Who was the "other" end?

a. Dixie Howell
b. Milt Gantenbein
c. Paul (Bear) Bryant
d. Max McGee
e. Bud Wilkinson
f. Tarzan White

Prior to the coin flip that began the first sudden death overtime period of the 1962 AFL championship game, Dallas Texans coach Hank Stram instructed captain Abner Haynes to opt for kicking off with the scoreboard clock at the Texans' backs, i.e. with the wind. In the pressure and confusion, Haynes, upon winning the toss, told the referee, "We'll kick to the clock." With that statement, Haynes in effect (however unwittingly) had attempted to exercise two options rather than the one he was allowed. Thus, "We'll kick" became Haynes's only choice, forcing Dallas to kick into the wind and taking away the advantage gained by winning the coin toss. The Texans overcame the mistake, however, and beat Houston 20–17 on a field goal by Tommy Brooker three minutes into the second overtime period.

35. Vacation job

Which former major league baseball manager quarter-backed George Halas's first pro team, the Decatur Staleys, in 1920?

   a. Casey Stengel
   b. Hugo Bezdek
   c. Charlie Dressen
   d. Walt Alston
   e. Earl Weaver
   f. Eddie Stanky

36. Mammal house

Name the seven NFL teams with animal nicknames.

As a youngster, Chicago Bears wide receiver Brian Baschnagel attended 19 different schools in 12 years.

37. The war experience helped

Name the former Marine Corps ace, Congressional Medal of Honor winner, and Governor of South Dakota who was the first AFL Commissioner.

a. Lamar Hunt
b. Joe Foss
c. Joe Robbie
d. Al Davis
e. Milt Woodard
f. Sid Gillman

38. Zip, zip

True or false? The 1961 and 1962 Green Bay Packers are the only teams to win back-to-back NFL championships by shutouts.

39. Tough act to follow

In his first at-bat as a major league baseball player, this Pro Football Hall of Famer set an American League record by getting a pinch-hit home run. Who is he?

a. Carroll Hardy
b. Sid Luckman
c. Ken Strong
d. Clarence (Ace) Parker
e. Johnny Mize
f. Paddy Driscoll

40. Who could forget?

Most NFL history buffs know that the Chicago Bears defeated the Washington Redskins 73–0 in the 1940 championsip game. However, the two teams had met three weeks prior to the championship game. What was the outcome of the earlier meeting?

a. Washington 73, Chicago 0.
b. Washington 7, Chicago 7
c. Washington 7, Chicago 3
d. Chicago 7, Washington 3
e. Chicago 21, Washington 20
f. Chicago 73, Washington 0

41. Having it both ways

Identify the only coach in pro football history to win world championships in both the AFL and NFL.

a. Weeb Ewbank
b. John Madden
c. Chuck Noll
d. Tom Landry
e. Wally Lemm
f. Ray Flaherty

42. Collection plate

Who is the former Rams fullback who used his NFL salary to finance his divinity school education?

   a. Deacon Jones
   b. Deacon Dan Towler
   c. Deacon Turner
   d. Vilnis Ezerins
   e. Don Perkins
   f. Preacher Pilot

43. It only *seemed* like the whole year

The last 0–0 tie in the NFL was between the Detroit Lions and the New York Giants. In what year was the game played?

   a. 1967
   b. 1931
   c. 1958
   d. 1943
   e. 1979
   f. 1952

44. Javelin catcher

True or false? Mike Fuller is the all-time NFL leader for punt return average with 11.5 yards per return.

The starting center for the Cleveland Browns when they defeated Detroit 56–10 for the 1954 NFL championship was Frank Gatski. The starting center for the Detroit Lions when they defeated Cleveland 59–14 for the 1957 NFL championship was Frank Gatski.

45. High and deep

True or false? Horace Gillom of the Cleveland Browns compiled the highest career punting average (43.8 yards) in NFL history.

46. Throwing with the right side of the brain

Who is considered the first prominent lefthanded quarterback in the pros?

   a. Benny Freidman
   b. Frankie Albert
   c. Ken Stabler
   d. Bob Waterfield
   e. Jim Del Gaizo
   f. Tommy Thompson

Gary Campbell, former Chicago Bears outside linebacker, is a native of Hawaii. His middle name is Kalani. His daughter's is Kealiialohiokalani, which means My Shining Princess from Heaven.

47. Now, the bad news

True or false? At first it was thought that St. Louis Cardinals rookie Roy Green had set an NFL kickoff return record with a 108-yard return in 1979 against the Dallas Cowboys, but later the return yardage was officially revised downward to 106, which tied him with Al Carmichael of the Packers and Noland Smith of the Chiefs.

48. Man on a string

Which player returned more than 500 kicks (235 punt returns, 275 kickoff returns) during his 10-year career?

   a. Ron Smith
   b. Abe Woodson
   c. George McAfee
   d. Dick Bass
   e. Dick Hoak
   f. Mike Nelms

49. Hard work

True or false? In 1975 Chuck Foreman accomplished the "triple crown" by leading the NFC in scoring, receiving, and rushing.

50. Favorite sons

Match the 1983 all-pro player in the first column with the college he attended in the second column.

OFFENSE

1. Roy Green, WR	a. Minnesota
2. Mike Quick, WR	b. Alabama
3. Todd Christensen, TE	c. Notre Dame
4. Anthony Munoz, T	d. Pittsburgh
5. Keith Fahnhorst, T	e. Brigham Young
6. Russ Grimm, G	f. SMU
7. John Hannah, G	g. Henderson State
8. Mike Webster, C	h. USC
9. Eric Dickerson, RB	i. Kansas
10. John Riggins, RB	j. North Carolina State
11. Joe Theismann, QB	k. Wisconsin

DEFENSE

1. Doug Betters, DE	a. Maryland
2. Howie Long, DE	b. UCLA
3. Randy White, DT	c. Baylor
4. Doug English, DT	d. Colgate
5. Jack Lambert, LB	e. Nevada-Reno
6. Lawrence Taylor, LB	f. Grambling
7. Chip Banks, LB	g. Texas
8. Gary Green, CB	h. North Carolina
9. Everson Walls, CB	i. Kent State
10. Kenny Easley, S	j. Villanova
11. Mark Murphy, S	k. USC

51. "Outlined against . . ."

Which of the famous Notre Dame "Four Horsemen" served as the NFL's first commissioner?

52. Throwing 'em where they ain't

Which quarterback established an NFL single-season record by being intercepted only once in 151 attempts?

- a. Bart Starr
- b. Joe Ferguson
- c. Milt Plum
- d. Ron Jaworski
- e. Dan Marino
- f. Jim Hardy

53. Over the table

True or false? The first known incident of a player's receiving money to play football was in 1892, when the Allegheny Athletic Association of Pittsburgh paid William (Pudge) Heffelfinger $500 for a game.

54. Isn't he from . . . ?

Match the NFL player in the first column with the school he attended in the second column.

BIG TEN

1. Mike Pruitt
2. Chris Hinton
3. Reggie Roby
4. Babe Luufenberg
5. Butch Woolfolk
6. Brad Van Pelt
7. Tom Cousineau
8. Doug Dieken
9. Mike Webster
10. Elmer Bailey

a. Indiana
b. Iowa
c. Michigan State
d. Michigan
e. Illinois
f. Ohio State
g. Wisconsin
h. Northwestern
i. Minnesota
j. Purdue

PAC-10

1. Marcus Allen
2. Freeman McNeil
3. Chuck Muncie
4. James Lofton
5. Blair Bush
6. Jack Thompson
7. Russ Francis
8. Dennis Boyd
9. John Jefferson
10. Ricky Hunley

a. Arizona
b. Arizona State
c. Oregon
d. Oregon State
e. Washington
f. Washington State
g. Stanford
h. California
i. UCLA
j. USC

BIG EIGHT

1. Greg Pruitt
2. Dexter Manley
3. Larry Brown
4. Steve Grogan
5. Pete Brock
6. Kenny Neil
7. Tony Galbreath
8. Andra Franklin

a. Colorado
b. Oklahoma
c. Oklahoma State
d. Kansas
e. Missouri
f. Kansas State
g. Iowa State
h. Nebraska

SOUTHWESTERN CONFERENCE

1. Jerry Sisemore
2. Curtis Dickey
3. Thomas Howard
4. Wilson Whitley
5. Mike Renfro
6. Eric Dickerson
7. Joe Ferguson
8. Walter Abercrombie
9. Tommy Kramer

a. Rice
b. Baylor
c. Texas
d. Texas A&M
e. Texas Tech
f. Texas Christian
g. Houston
h. Arkansas
i. Southern Methodist

SOUTHEASTERN CONFERENCE

1. Tony Nathan
2. Lindsay Scott
3. William Andrews
4. Jack Reynolds
5. Ben Williams
6. A.J. Duhe
7. Johnie Cooks
8. Wes Chandler
9. Dennis Harrison
10. Art Still

a. Mississippi
b. Alabama
c. Vanderbilt
d. Georgia
e. Mississippi State
f. Auburn
g. Kentucky
h. Louisiana State
i. Tennessee
j. Florida

INDEPENDENTS

1. Tom Jackson
2. Curt Warner
3. Tony Dorsett
4. Joe Theismann
5. Mark Murphy
6. George Rogers
7. Ottis Anderson
8. Art Monk
9. Darryl Talley
10. Joe Klecko

a. Pittsburgh
b. Temple
c. Colgate
d. Louisville
e. South Carolina
f. West Virginia
g. Miami
h. Notre Dame
i. Syracuse
j. Penn State

Contrary to modern popular thought, the first game between the NFL and the AFL took place in 1926. The New York Giants of the NFL defeated the Philadelphia Quakers 31–0. The first AFL was a league designed to showcase the talents of Red Grange.

55. Eclipsed

Which Pro Football Hall of Fame inductee was Babe Ruth's predecessor as the New York Yankees' right fielder?

    a. Lou Gehrig
    b. George Halas
    c. Paddy Driscoll
    d. Ace Parker
    e. Bobby Layne
    f. Evar Swanson

56. Part of the "baby boom"

Name the original eight teams of the All-America Football Conference of 1946.

The drop-kick made its final appearance in the NFL championship game of 1941, when Ray (Scooter) McLean scored the final point of the afternoon for the Chicago Bears in their 37–9 victory over the New York Giants.

57. Hands like leather

By carrying the ball on 390 attempts in 1983, he broke the NFL record for carries in one season. Name the running back.

  a. Earl Campbell
  b. Eric Dickerson
  c. Walter Payton
  d. John Riggins
  e. Chuck Muncie
  f. Curt Warner

58. Many happy returns

True or false? Lynn Chandnois, who played with the Pittsburgh Steelers from 1950–56, is the all-time NFL kickoff return leader with an average of 29.6 yards per return.

59. Cornerstones

Which two members of Fordham University's famous line of the 1930s, "The Seven Blocks of Granite," are in the Pro Football Hall of Fame?

  a. Vince Lombardi and Alex Wojciechowicz
  b. Vince Lombardi and Ed Franco
  c. Glenn Davis and Doc Blanchard
  d. Bulldog Turner and Dan Fortmann
  e. Vince Lombardi and Phil Bengtson
  f. Steve Filipowicz and Alex Wojciechowicz

60. Probing the legend

True or false? The 1960 Philadelphia Eagles, coached by Buck Shaw, were the only team to defeat Vince Lombardi's Green Bay Packers in a championship game.

61. Keep your head down

Who holds the NFL career record for highest field goal percentage?

- a. Rolf Benirschke
- b. Don Crockroft
- c. Tom Dempsey
- d. Rafael Septien
- e. Mark Moseley
- f. Garo Yepremian

62. Some other guy

Who broke Jim Brown's NFL record for most 100-yard games rushing?

- a. Franco Harris
- b. Archie Griffin
- c. Tony Dorsett
- d. O.J. Simpson
- e. Walter Payton
- f. Tony Canadeo

63. Not from around here

Before moving to Washington, what city did the Redskins call home?

   a. Atlanta
   b. Boston
   c. Chicago
   d. Detroit
   e. Easton
   f. Frankford

64. Courted, then netted

In the 1960s, the Dallas Cowboys, who have built a reputation for finding players in unorthodox places, fielded two starters who had played no college football but had been basketball players as collegians. Who were they?

   a. Walt Garrison and Chuck Howley
   b. Pete Gent and Mel Renfro
   c. Don Perkins and Cornell Green
   d. Walt Garrison and Mel Renfro
   e. Chuck Howley and Mel Renfro
   f. Pete Gent and Cornell Green

At the start of the 1979 NFL season, the San Diego Chargers' roster showed three names of former and present major league baseball players: running back Hank Bauer, quarterback Dave Rader, and center Bob Rush.

65. "The invisible team"

True of false? There are eight officials in an NFL crew.

66. *Now*, may we go home?

Who kicked the field goal in the second overtime period to win the 1962 AFL title for the Dallas Texans?

- a. George Blanda
- b. Abner Haynes
- c. Lamar Hunt
- d. Lou Groza
- e. Tommy Brooker
- f. Bill Shockley

The first televised pro football game took place on October 22, 1939 at Brooklyn's Ebbets Field. The Brooklyn Dodgers defeated the Philadelphia Eagles 23–14, and the game was carried by NBC, which used two cameras, one at field level and one on the mezzanine. Announcer Allan (Skip) Walz was his own spotter and used hand signals to direct the cameraman to the appropriate game action.

67. A lost art

Which member of the Pro Football Hall of Fame is considered "the last of the great drop-kickers?"

    a. Lou Groza
    b. George Blanda
    c. Dutch Clark
    d. Jim Bakken
    e. Sammy Baugh
    f. Doak Walker

68. Let's see, that's three gallons of blue . . .

Name the former NFL general manager who, as a player, designed the first helmet logo—for the Los Angeles Rams in 1948—then painted the team's entire supply of headgear.

    a. Bob Waterfield
    b. Bucko Kilroy
    c. Fred Gehrke
    d. Norm Van Brocklin
    e. Jim Finks
    f. Bobby Beathard

69. Receptive

Who holds the NFL career record for most receptions?

    a. Raymond Berry
    b. Don Maynard
    c. Lionel Taylor
    d. Dan Abramowicz
    e. Charley Taylor
    f. Charlie Joiner

70. Pickpocket

True or false? Emlen Tunnell, who played with the New York Giants and Green Bay Packers, is the all-time NFL interception leader.

71. They "used him up"

Which running back holds the NFL record for the most rushing attempts in a game, 43?

    a. James Wilder, Buccaneers
    b. Earl Campbell, Oilers
    c. O.J. Simpson, 49ers
    d. John Riggins, Redskins
    e. Butch Woolfolk, Giants
    f. Harry Newman, Giants

72. Without starting blocks

Identify the former Olympic gold medal-winning sprinter who once scored on a 101-yard interception return.

   a. Bob Hayes
   b. Ollie Matson
   c. Homer Jones
   d. Doak Walker
   e. Henry Carr
   f. Gerald Tinker

73. The human pendulum

Name the kicker who holds the NFL record for most field goals in a season, 34.

   a. Lou Michaels
   b. Sonny Jurgensen
   c. Jack Manders
   d. Jim Turner
   e. Roy Gerela
   f. Ward Cuff

74. Me DEE-fense

Name the former NFL linebacker who played Tarzan in films in the 1960s.

a. Buster Crabbe
b. Burt Reynolds
c. Lee Majors
d. Mike Henry
e. Tim Rossovich
f. Johnny Mack Brown

Don't be fooled by this bogus trivia question: In 1963, the most valuable players of the National Football League, the American Football League, and baseball's American and National Leagues all wore the same number. What was it? Well, it wasn't one number. The bogus answer is 32, which was in fact the number worn by Jim Brown (NFL), Elston Howard (AL), and Sandy Koufax (NL). But the AFL's most valuable player, Clem Daniels of the Oakland Raiders, wore 36. Tough question, though.

75. No. 1 in their hearts

Which jersey number was issued to O.J. Simpson when he reported to the Buffalo Bills in 1969?

    a. 32
    b. 9
    c. 00
    d. 36
    e. 7
    f. 30

76. Spiral showcase

The NFL record for longest punt (98 yards) may never be broken. Who holds it?

    a. Sammy Baugh
    b. Yale Lary
    c. Horace Gillom
    d. Tom Blanchard
    e. Steve O'Neal
    f. Tommy Davis

The first player to use eyeglasses during an NFL game was Baltimore receiver Raymond Berry, who wore shaded swimmer's goggles to protect against the winter sun in the Los Angeles Coliseum in the late 1950s and early 1960s.

77. Air travel

Which relatively unheralded young quarterback passed for more than 4,000 yards in 1983?

- a. Dave Kreig
- b. Mike Pagel
- c. Steve Dils
- d. Eric Hipple
- e. Bill Kenney
- f. Scott Brunner

78. Key player

Name the former Pro Bowl defensive tackle who retired abruptly in 1974 to devote full time to his career as a pianist/songwriter?

- a. Merlin Olsen
- b. Bob Lilly
- c. Mike Reid
- d. Bill Kollar
- e. Willie Lanier
- f. Jethro Pugh

79. Rip and run

Which defensive back holds the career record for returning interceptions for the most career touchdowns (9)?

a. Lem Barney
b. Ken Houston
c. Jack Butler
d. Dick (Night Train) Lane
e. Will Sherman
f. Milt Davis

80. Track meet

The highest scoring game in NFL history was played in 1966 between the Washington Redskins and the New York Giants. What was the score?

a. 73–0
b. 47–45
c. 101–28
d. 68–14
e. 86–21
f. 72–41

81. Dodge 'em

True or false? In 1979 Rick Upchurch of the Broncos surpassed Emlen Tunnell as the NFL's all-time leader for punt return yardage (2,288).

82. No stopping him

The record for the most points scored by an individual in an NFL game (40) has stood since 1929. Who holds the record?

   a. George Halas
   b. Ernie Nevers
   c. Dub Jones
   d. Dutch Clark
   e. Clarke Hinkle
   f. Hinkey Haines

83. Complementary

True or false? Jim and Jack Youngblood, both formerly, of the Rams, are the only twins playing in the NFL.

84. Fast break

Who was the first NFL running back to rush for more than a thousand yards in each of his first three seasons?

   a. Franco Harris
   b. O.J. Simpson
   c. Walter Payton
   d. John Brockington
   e. Larry Brown
   f. Byron (Whizzer) White

The term "Red Dog," the original nickname for the defensive gambit now known as the blitz, came from the first man to attempt one: Don (Red) Ettinger, a linebacker for the New York Giants from 1948–50. With the offensive team in a third-and-long situation, Ettinger left his normal position and sacked the quarterback for a substantial loss. "I had red hair, and I was just doggin' the quarterback a little," he explained later.

85. Popular title

True or false? The American Football League (1960–69) was the fourth NFL rival to be so named.

86. Back it up

Name the NFL running back who was credited with a 1,000-yard season after a review of films showed that what had been called lost yardage was really a fumble and should not have been subtracted from his total.

a. Mercury Morris
b. Duane Thomas
c. Larry Csonka
d. O.J. Simpson
e. Jim Kiick
f. Don Perkins

The first President of the United States to attend a Monday Night Football game was Jimmy Carter, who watched Washington defeat Dallas 9–5 in 1978.

87. Extra credit for "Wahoo"

Match the player in the first columns with his nickname in the second column.

1.	Red Grange	a.	The Dancing Bear
2.	Ted Hendricks	b.	Turk
3.	Alex Karras	c.	Mad Duck
4.	Elroy Hirsch	d.	The Mad Stork
5.	Clyde Turner	e.	Bruiser
6.	Ron McDole	f.	The Lion
7.	Frank Kinard	g.	The Galloping Ghost
8.	Daryle Lamonica	h.	Crazylegs
9.	Leo Nomellini	i.	The Mad Bomber
10.	Glenn Edwards	j.	Bulldog

88. The aviary

Name the four NFL teams with bird nicknames.

89. Double centuries

Name the player who recorded more 200-yard games rushing (six) than any other running back in NFL history.

    a. Walter Payton
    b. William Andrews
    c. O.J. Simpson
    d. Jim Brown
    e. Earl Campbell
    f. Billy Sims

90. Going the extra mile

Who are the only NFL running backs to gain more than 2,000 yards rushing in a season?

    a. Ottis Anderson and O.J. Simpson
    b. Jim Brown and Walter Payton
    c. Franco Harris and Jim Brown
    d. Earl Campbell and Walter Payton
    e. Walter Payton and Eric Dickerson
    f. O.J. Simpson and Eric Dickerson

91. Taking the bitter with the sweet

Which quarterback once held the NFL records for most touchdown passes (36) in a season and most interceptions in a season (42)?

    a. Greg Cook
    b. Ken Anderson
    c. George Blanda
    d. Fran Tarkenton
    e. Norman Snead
    f. Sid Luckman

92. Home of champions

Which team has won the most NFL championships?

   a. Chicago Bears
   b. Green Bay Packers
   c. Dallas Cowboys
   d. Canton Bulldogs
   e. Detroit Lions
   f. Atlanta Falcons

93. Reigning runner

Which running back led the NFL in rushing in 1983?

   a. Marcus Allen
   b. Walter Payton
   c. Ottis Anderson
   d. Curt Warner
   e. Eric Dickerson
   f. Tony Dorsett

94. That'll cost you . . .

Which team was assessed the most penalty yardage in one game, 209?

   a. Atlanta Falcons
   b. Baltimore Colts
   c. Cleveland Browns
   d. Dallas Cowboys
   e. Philadelphia Eagles
   f. Frankford Yellowjackets

95. "It's up, it's . . ."

Who holds the NFL record for the longest field goal?

a. Bruce Alford
b. Lou Groza
c. Paddy Driscoll
d. Tom Dempsey
e. Jack Manders
f. Gene Mingo

Earl Morrall was acquired by the Baltimore Colts for the 1968 season as an "insurance" quarterback. Johnny Unitas was injured during much of the regular season. Morrall started against, and beat, each of his former teams that season:

Colts 27, San Francisco 10
Colts 41, Pittsburgh 7
Colts 42, San Francisco 14
Colts 26, New York Giants 0
Colts 27, Detroit 10

96. Born to lose

Which NFL team lost the most consecutive games?

a. Detroit Lions
b. New Orleans Saints
c. San Francisco 49ers
d. Philadelphia Eagles
e. Los Angeles Rams
f. Tampa Bay Buccaneers

97. The last of the great quintuple-threats

Who holds the NFL record for the most combined yards gained (rushing, receiving, punt returns, kickoff returns, and fumble returns) in a season?

a. Bruce Harper
b. Timmy Brown
c. Terry Metcalf
d. Mack Herron
e. Bobby Mitchell
f. James Brooks

Walter Payton's marriage gave him another bond with his college (Jackson State) teammate and best friend, Rickey Young. Young's wife Hazel and Mrs. Payton (Connie) are aunt and niece, making Young Payton's uncle by marriage.

98. Pioneer

Who was the first modern-day black quarterback in the NFL?

a. Marlin Briscoe
b. Eldridge Dickey
c. Joe Gilliam
d. Willie Thrower
e. James Harris
f. Doug Williams

99. You gotta be a football hero

Who is the baseball player and manager who was a star runner at Louisiana State in the 1940s while Pro Football Hall of Famer Steve Van Buren was used as a blocking back?

a. Charlie Conerly
b. Alvin Dark
c. Lloyd Merriman
d. Casey Stengel
e. Vic Janowicz
f. Bill Dickey

100. Gift of prophecy

Jeanne Dixon, a noted pyschic, is the sister of which famous football player?

a. Bob Waterfield
b. Bobby Layne
c. Hewritt Dixon
d. Paul Dickson
e. Cliff Battles
f. Erny Pinckert

101. Stay tuned

Which linebacker had a role in an episode of the daytime drama (they used to call them soap operas) "One Life to Live"?

a. Jack Lambert
b. Matt Millen
c. E.J. Junior
d. Greg Buttle
e. Brad Van Pelt
f. Harry Carson

102. Made to be broken

Which quarterback broke the NFL records for the most passing attempts and completions in a season in 1981?

a. Dan Fouts
b. Danny White
c. Jim Hart
d. Terry Bradshaw
e. Archie Manning
f. Jim Zorn

103. Mr. Consistency

Who holds the record for most times leading the NFL in rushing?

a. O.J. Simpson
b. Walter Payton
c. Jim Brown
d. Tony Canadeo
e. Steve Van Buren
f. Bill Paschal

104. Packing the pigskin to paydirt

Which Pro Football Hall of Fame halfback/flanker holds the record for scoring a touchdown in 18 consecutive games?

    a. Jim Brown
    b. Jim Taylor
    c. Gale Sayers
    d. Hugh McElhenny
    e. Don Hutson
    f. Lenny Moore

105. Just sign here, son

Who were the two Dallas Cowboys stars signed to personal services contracts and dealt for, rather than drafted, in 1960?

    a. Eddie LeBaron and Bill Howton
    b. Bob Lilly and Bob Hayes
    c. Don Perkins and Don Meredith
    d. Lee Roy Jordan and Jerry Tubbs
    e. Amos Marsh and Mel Renfro
    f. Frank Clarke and Chuck Howley

In 1957 the Philadelphia Eagles drafted the following players:

   Round 1, Clarence Peaks, Michigan State.
   Round 2, Billy Ray Barnes, Wake Forest.
   Round 3, Tommy McDonald, Oklahoma.
   Round 4, Sonny Jurgensen, Duke.

In the early 1960s, the quartet comprised the starting backfield, with Jurgensen at quarterback, Barnes at half-back, Peaks at fullback, and McDonald at flanker.

106. When in doubt . . .

Which punter failed prior tryouts with the New York Jets, but made it with the Kansas City Chiefs in 1979 and led the NFL in punting?

   a. Steve O'Neal
   b. Jerrel Wilson
   c. Bucky Dilts
   d. Chuck Ramsey
   e. Zenon Andrusyshyn
   f. Bob Grupp

107. Something to kick about

Which NFL umpire shares the record for kicking the most extra points (nine) in a game?

a. Frank Sinkovitz
b. Jim Tunney
c. Dean Look
d. Lou Groza
e. Pat Harder
f. Tommy Davis

While playing quarterback in the NFL, Charley Johnson and Frank Ryan earned Ph.D.s: Johnson's was in chemical engineering, Ryan's in mathematics.

108. Draft-dodgers

The Washington Redskins chose Art Monk, a wide receiver from Syracuse, on the first round of the 1980 draft. It was the first time in years that they had kept their number one pick. Who had been their last first round choice?

a. Ray McDonald, 1967
b. Jim (Yazoo) Smith, 1968
c. Bill Brundige, 1970
d. Moses Denson, 1972
e. Mike Thomas, 1975
f. John Riggins, 1976

109. If it's moving, fall on it

Who holds the record for the most opponents' fumbles recovered in a season?

a. Corwin Clatt
b. Chuck Howley
c. Don Hultz
d. Joe Schmidt
e. Dick Butkus
f. Jim Marshall

110. They shall pass

Which was the first team in NFL history to attempt more than 600 passes?

   a. New York Giants, 1961
   b. Dallas Cowboys, 1967
   c. Green Bay Packers, 1936
   d. San Francisco 49ers, 1979
   e. Houston Oilers, 1965
   f. New York Jets, 1968

111. Ground pounders

Which is the only team to have four players gain more than 500 yards rushing in the same season?

   a. New England Patriots, 1978
   b. Pittsburgh Steelers, 1976
   c. Detroit Lions, 1974
   d. Green Bay Packers, 1961
   e. Miami Dolphins, 1972
   f. Los Angeles Raiders, 1983

112. Super coverage

True or false? Super Bowl I was televised by two networks, ABC and NBC.

113. Tool of ignorance

What was the nickname of the Kansas City Chiefs' defensive back who predicted dire results for the Packers in Super Bowl I?

a. Brother Sledge
b. The Hatchet
c. Stinger
d. Motor Mouth
e. The Hammer
f. Crash

114. On his toes

Who kicked four field goals to help the Green Bay Packers win Super Bowl II?

a. Paul Hornung
b. Jerry Kramer
c. Don Chandler
d. Mike Eischeid
e. Jim Taylor
f. Ron Widby

115. Holding on to it

Name the man who shares the record for the most touch-downs in a Super Bowl game, having caught two scoring passes in Super Bowl II.

- a. Glenn Bass
- b. Bill Miller
- c. Harry Schuh
- d. Chuck Mercein
- e. Bob Long
- f. Bob Tucker

116. Audacity spoken here

True or false? Except for the Green Bay Packers in Super Bowl I, the New York Jets are the only team to win a Super Bowl game in their first attempt.

Chicago Bears linebacker Brian Cabral is of Hawaiian descent. His original surname is Kealiihaaheo.

117. Out of sight

Near the end of the first half of Super Bowl III, quarterback Earl Morrall of the Baltimore Colts had a receiver wide open in the end zone on a gadget play. Morrall did not see him and attempted to throw to a closer man. The ball was intercepted. Who was the man left standing in the end zone, waving his arms?

- a. Tom Matte
- b. Randy Beverly
- c. Jimmy Orr
- d. John Mackey
- e. George Sauer, Jr.
- f. Pettis Norman

118. Masochist

True or false? Fran Tarkenton was the starting quarterback in all four of the Minnesota Vikings' Super Bowl losses.

Throughout his career Johnny Unitas's flattop haircut and high-top shoes were as much trademarks as his jersey number 19. For Super Bowl V, Unitas presented a new image—long hair and low-cut shoes.

119. Mumbo jumbo

Kansas City head coach Hank Stram had a special name for the multiple offensive formations he used in Super Bowl IV. What was it?

   a. The 65 Toss Power Trap Series
   b. The Belly Series
   c. The Offense of the Seventies
   d. The Bazooka
   e. The Peg-leg T
   f. The Kansas City Strip

120. Helping hand

A long touchdown reception in Super Bowl V was a controversial one. It was ruled that a Dallas defender tipped the ball after it had been touched by the original intended receiver (Eddie Hinton) but before John Mackey caught it to complete the 75-yard play. Name the defensive back who was ruled to have touched the ball.

   a. Mel Renfro
   b. Tom Maxwell
   c. Cornell Green
   d. Charlie Waters
   e. Herb Adderley
   f. Rick Volk

121. Silent partner

Although he did not win player of the game honors, which running back had an outstanding day (19 carries for 95 yards and one touchdown) for the winners of Super Bowl VI?

   a. Jim Kiick
   b. Duane Thomas
   c. Larry Csonka
   d. Walt Garrison
   e. Robert Newhouse
   f. Mercury Morris

122. Out-of-town dudes

Both of Roger Staubach's touchdown passes in Super Bowl VI were caught by players who had spent the majority of their careers with teams other than the Cowboys. Name the pair of not-so-old cowhands.

   a. Paul Warfield and Billy Howton
   b. Gloster Richardson and Billy Truax
   c. Tommy McDonald and Ron Sellers
   d. Lance Alworth and Mike Ditka
   e. Margene Adkins and Richmond Flowers
   f. Reggie Rucker and Halvor Hagen

123. Peak performance

Which defensive lineman had a "once-in-a-lifetime" game in Super Bowl VII?

   a. Manny Sistrunk
   b. Otis Sistrunk
   c. Bob Heinz
   d. Manny Fernandez
   e. Larry Ball
   f. John Wilbur

124. Not in the playbook

Field goal placements usually follow a certain format: snap, hold, kick. In Super Bowl VII, Garo Yepremian, the Dolphins' kicker, did something that made the game more exciting. What was it?

   a. He kicked barefooted.
   b. After a blocked field goal attempt, he attempted a pass that turned into a fumble and was run back for a Redskins touchdown.
   c. He drop-kicked a 43-yard field goal.
   d. He kicked one extra point with his right foot and another with his left.
   e. He ran for an extra point after faking a kick.
   f. He passed for an extra point.

125. A ring for each finger

True or false? Marv Fleming is the only man to play in five Super Bowls—I and II with the Packers, and VI, VII, and VIII with the Dolphins.

126. Grounded

Rushing was the key to winning Super Bowl IX. The Steelers gained 249 yards on the ground, while the Vikings managed considerably fewer. What was the Vikings' net rushing yardage?

    a. Minus-47 yards
    b. 117 yards
    c. 187 yards
    d. 17 yards
    e. 44 yards
    f. 93 yards.

One player not disturbed by media attention accompanying Super Bowl IX was Pittsburgh Steelers center Ray Mansfield. Said the 33-year-old veteran of the Steelers' lean years, "I've been in this league for twelve seasons, and no one's ever asked me a question."

127. Understudies

Two of the Steelers' all-pro linebackers—Andy Russell and Jack Lambert—missed much of Super Bowl IX due to injuries. Which two young linebackers took their places?

a. Loren Toews and Ed Bradley
b. Mike Webster and Marv Kellum
c. Jack Ham and Marv Kellum
d. Dick Conn and Jim Allen
e. Reggie Harrison and Robin Cole
f. Doug Fisher and Ray May

128. Reeling with excitement

Which movie used Super Bowl X as a backdrop?

a. Bad Day at Black Rock
b. Black Sunday
c. Semi-Tough
d. North Dallas Forty
e. The Longest Yard
f. Crazylegs II

President Richard M. Nixon, whose Florida "White House" was located at Key Biscayne, sent Dolphins head coach Don Shula a play for use in Super Bowl VI. The following year Nixon sent a play to George Allen of the Redskins even though the Dolphins were again in the Super Bowl. Nixon claimed that the Redskins were "really my 'home team.' "

129. Journeyman

True or false? Preston Pearson has appeared in five Super Bowls with five different teams: Colts, Vikings, Steelers, Chiefs, and Cowboys.

130. Magnetizer

True or false? Though he scored no touchdowns in Super Bowl XI, Fred Biletnikoff's four receptions for 79 yards earned him the game's most valuable player award.

131. Icing

Which defensive back returned an interception 75 yards for a touchdown to give Oakland its final points in Super Bowl XI?

a. Jack Tatum
b. George Atkinson
c. Willie Brown
d. Alonzo (Skip) Thomas
e. Neal Colzie
f. Nate Allen

132. Maiden voyage

True or false? Red Miller took the Denver Broncos to Super Bowl XII in his first year as head coach of the team.

133. X's and O's going everywhere

Which "gadget play" gave the Dallas Cowboys their final touchdown in Super Bowl XII?

a. A Statue of Liberty play with Tony Dorsett going 43 yards.
b. A running back-option pass from Robert Newhouse to Golden Richards.
c. A 27-yard pass from holder Danny White to field goal kicker Efren Herrera.
d. A Staubach-to-Dorsett-to-Preston-Pearson-to-Dorsett-back-to-Staubach-to-DuPree flea-flicker.
e. A Dorsett-to-Staubach pass.
f. A 27-yard run by field goal kicker Efren Herrera.

134. Doomsday duo

What distinction do Harvey Martin and Randy White share?

   a. They are the only two defensive players to receive Super Bowl most valuable player honors.

   b. They are the only Cowboys to win Super Bowl most valuable player honors.

   c. They are the only players named co-most valuable players in a Super Bowl.

   d. They are the only two most valuable players who did not play quarterback.

   e. They both scored touchdowns on fumble returns in Super Bowl XII.

   f. They both started in Super Bowl XII as rookies.

135. Automatic milestone

True or false? Either team in Super Bowl XIII—the Pittsburgh Steelers or Dallas Cowboys—would have become the first to win three Super Bowls.

136. Easily bored

True or false? Larry Cole of the Dallas Cowboys has started three Super Bowls at three different positions.

For Super Bowl XIII, the catering service that contracted with the Orange Bowl ordered the following: four tons of hot dogs, 100 pounds of cheese, 30,000 hamburgers, 1,000 heads of cabbage for sauerkraut, four tons of ice, 15,000 gallons of soda, 1,500 pounds of french fries, 15,000 ice cream sandwiches, and 3,000 gallons of coffee.

137. Hanging on

True or false? The Steelers and Rams combined to set two records in Super Bowl XIV—most yards passing, both teams (503) and fewest fumbles, both teams (0).

138. Passing Parade

True or false? Nine of the Super Bowl most valuable player awards have been won by quarterbacks, but only Bart Starr and Terry Bradshaw have been back-to-back winners.

Larry Ball was a reserve linebacker with the Miami Dolphins in 1972 when they went 17–0 in 1972 (including a victory in Super Bowl VII) and with the Tampa Bay Buccaneers when they went 0–14 in 1976.

139. Shadow figure

Which of the following was the first Super Bowl most valuable player who was *not* a quarterback?

a. Jan Stenerud
b. Mercury Morris
c. Lynn Swann
d. Chuck Howley
e. Bob Lilly
f. Joe Greene

140. Running away with it

Which running backs are the only four to be named most valuable players in the Super Bowl?

a. Tony Dorsett, Franco Harris, Jake Scott, and John Riggins
b. Duane Thomas, Walt Garrison, Franco Harris, and Larry Csonka
c. Larry Csonka, Larry Brown, Duane Thomas, and Marcus Allen
d. Larry Csonka, Franco Harris, John Riggins, and Marcus Allen
e. Chuck Foreman, Jack Maitland, Tony Dorsett, and Mike Garrett
f. Franco Harris, Wendell Tyler, Ricky Patton, and Dave Osborn

141. Show-stoppers

True or false? The only defensive players to have received the Super Bowl's most valuable player award were members of the Dallas Cowboys.

142. Receivers, recipients

True or false? Lynn Swann and John Stallworth are the only two receivers to win most valuable player awards in the Super Bowl.

143. Tough talk

Who originated the quote "40 for 60," which means 40 men (the team) for 60 minutes (the length of a game)?

   a. Fran Tarkenton
   b. Ken Stabler
   c. Len Dawson
   d. Joe Kapp
   e. Terry Bradshaw
   f. Bart Starr

144. Mystery men

What do the following men have in common? Mike Mercer, Bill Miller, Tom Nowatzke, Mike Bass, Dwight White, Percy Howard, Stu Voigt, Mike Hegman, and Ron Smith.

   a. They were all free agents who made it to the Super Bowl.
   b. Each scored in a Super Bowl.
   c. They all played on losing Super Bowl teams.
   d. They all were released by one Super Bowl team and acquired by another.
   e. They all played college football at Grambling.
   f. They all played in three or more Super Bowls.

145. Two by two

True or false? The only two safeties recorded in Super Bowl history are both credited to Pittsburgh Steelers.

146. Repetitious

True or false? Vince Lombardi, Don Shula, Tom Landry, and Chuck Noll each won back-to-back Super Bowls.

Veteran NFL field judge Bob Wortman has officiated two Super Bowls (VI and XII) and two NCAA basketball finals (UCLA vs. Kentucky in 1975 and Indiana vs. Michigan in 1976).

147. Over-the-hill gang(s)?

True or false? George Allen is the only coach in NFL history to take two different teams to the Super Bowl.

148. Sticky fingers

True or false? The leading interceptor in Super Bowl history is a free safety.

It is safe to say that the Miami Dolphins' game plan for Super Bowl VIII stressed ball control. In their 24–7 victory over Minnesota, they scored on three of their first four possessions and at one point led 24–0. Dolphins running back Larry Csonka set a Super Bowl rushing record with 145 yards in 33 carries, and quarterback Bob Griese attempted only seven passes, completing six for 73 yards.

149. Sacrificial lamb

True or false? Tom Landry has been in more Super Bowls than any other head coach, but he also has lost more.

150. Flying north in winter

True or false? The Silverdome in Pontiac, Michigan, in 1982 was the first Super Bowl site outside the Los Angeles, Miami, or New Orleans areas.

You Make the Call

The job of officiating an NFL game is anything but trivial. Proof of this is always fresh in the mind. It's as recent as the last crucial playoff game, where a whole season can appear to hang on a single call. So if the sub-atomic-sized details of the rule book can take on such mighty significance, what are they doing in this sea of minutiae? The answer is part of the question: an eye for detail brings the game into sharper focus. Whether the data you're gathering *seems* important or not, it's always worth storing for possible future use. With that in mind, and with one hand on your penalty flag, pay close attention to the next 30 situations (all of which actually took place). Our thanks go to their author, Norm Schachter, a former NFL official and currently an observer of officials for the league. For an instantly replayed unraveling of the problems, turn to page 172.

1. Opening number

On the opening kickoff of a game between San Diego and Seattle, the Chargers' return man catches the ball in his end zone and fumbles it there after taking a step or two. The ball rolls out to the 2-yard line, where a San Diego teammate recovers it and runs to midfield before being tackled by a Seattle player. During the fumble, while the ball is on the 2, a San Diego player clips one of the Seahawks at the 8-yard line. What would you rule?

   a. San Diego's ball, first and 10 at the Chargers' 4.
   b. San Diego's ball, first and 10 at the Chargers' 1.
   c. Re-kick from the 50-yard line (penalize San Diego 15 yards and replay the kickoff).
   d. Safety against San Diego, Chargers kick off from their 20.

2. Good deed for the day?

Indianapolis has the ball on New England's 40-yard line, third down and 15. The Indianapolis quarterback throws a look-in pass to his tight end. The ball goes off the tight end's hands at New England's 30-yard line and pops right into the hands of a New England cornerback. He runs the interception back to Indianapolis's 20, and the Indianapolis quarterback is the only man left who can tackle the runner. The cornerback avoids the quarterback but slips and falls without being touched. A New England teammate running alongside to block sees the cornerback slip. He reaches over and helps the ball carrier to his feet at Indianapolis's 20-yard line. He then blocks the Colts' quarterback at the 10-yard line, allowing the cornerback to go in for a score. How would you rule?

a. Touchdown.
b. New England's ball, first down at Indianapolis's 35-yard line.
c. New England's ball, first down at Indianapolis's 25-yard line.
d. New England's ball, first down at Indianapolis's 15-yard line.

3. This will only take a second

Dallas has the ball on its own 4-yard line, second down and 15. The Cowboys' quarterback hands off to his running back, who fumbles. The ball rolls backward, into Dallas's end zone. A Detroit defensive tackle pushes the Cowboys' quarterback out of the way, and a Lions' teammate recovers the ball in the end zone. How would you rule?

a. Touchdown for Detroit.
b. Touchback for Dallas.
c. Dallas's ball, first down at its own 9-yard line (after penalizing Detroit five yards from the spot of the previous snap for illegal use of hands).
d. Dallas's ball, first down at its own 19-yard line (after penalizing Detroit 15 yards from the spot of the previous snap for illegal use of hands).

4. Echoes of another era

Dallas leads the New York Giants by two points with a minute left to play. The Giants' placekicker prepares for a field goal attempt from the Dallas 12-yard line. As he kicks the ball with his right foot, a Dallas defensive tackle comes crashing through and blocks the ball with his chest. The ball bounces back to the kicker's left, and as it bounces, he kicks it with his left foot. It goes over the crossbar, and the crowd goes wild. The official blows his whistle and throws his flag. The players rush him and ask why. He says, "I don't know what it is, but I know it's wrong." A few seconds later, he announces his decision. Which of these rulings should it be?

a. Field goal.
b. Touchback.
c. Penalize the Giants 15 yards from the spot of the snap.
d. Penalize the Giants 15 yards from the spot of the second kick.

5. The old greased pig play

Washington has the ball, third down and 14, on its own 4-yard line. The Redskins' quarterback fakes a handoff to his running back, then drops back into his own end zone. He is blindsided by a Dallas tackler, and the ball pops out of his hands. The ball scoots toward the sideline and is angling out of the end zone. It reaches Washington's 1-yard line when the Redskins' running back tries to fall on it, but it squirts away and hits the shaft of the goal line marker. A Dallas player then falls on the ball in the end zone. What would you rule?

    a. Touchdown for Dallas.
    b. Safety against Washington.
    c. Touchback for Washington.
    d. Washington's ball on its own 1-yard line, fourth down.

6. Not part of the script

San Francisco has the ball on its own 15-yard line, second down and 15. The 49ers' quarterback rolls out and looks downfield for an eligible receiver. He is being chased, and he runs past the line of scrimmage to his 16-yard line, where he tries to throw a backward pass to his running back. The pass goes forward instead of backward. An Eagles linebacker bats the ball back toward the 49ers' end zone. The ball lands in the end zone, where the linebacker falls on it. What would you rule?

  a. Touchdown.
  b. 49ers' ball, first and 10 from their 31.
  c. 49ers' ball, third and 19 from their 11.
  d. 49ers' ball, third and 15 from their 15.

7. Flying low

Atlanta has just scored. With less than two minutes to go, the Falcons now trail the New York Jets by only two points. The Atlanta kicker attempts an onside kick, but the ball goes only eight yards before being touched by a Jets player. The ball then is touched, in turn, by an Atlanta player, a Jets player, and another Atlanta player. It is finally recovered by an Atlanta player on the Falcons' 45-yard line, with one of his feet touching the sideline at the 46. How would you rule it?

    a. Atlanta's ball on its own 45.
    b. Atlanta's ball on its own 46.
    c. Re-kick with a five-yard penalty against Atlanta.
    d. Jets' ball on Atlanta's 45-yard line.

8. Overjoyed

Minnesota is having trouble moving the ball against Detroit. It is third down for the Vikings at their own 10-yard line. The Vikings' quarterback scrambles around in his backfield and finally unloads a long pass to his wide receiver, who catches the ball at midfield. The receiver runs toward Detroit's goal line. When he reaches the Lions' 5, he mistakes it for the goal line. He spikes the ball from the 5. It hits on the 4 and rolls into Detroit's end zone, where a Detroit player falls on it. How would you rule it?

   a. Award a touchback to Detroit.
   b. Minnesota's ball on Detroit's 5-yard line, first down.
   c. Minnesota's ball on Detroit's 10-yard line, first down.
   d. Minnesota's ball on Detroit's 10-yard line, second down.

9. Lost in traffic

The Chicago Bears have the ball on third down at midfield. A Bears' running back takes a handoff and runs to the Vikings' 40-yard line, where he fumbles into a crowd of players. A Minnesota player picks up the ball but, due to confusion, runs toward his own goal line. Just as he crosses the goal line, he throws the ball down in front of himself. The ball hits in the end zone and bounces out to the Minnesota 2-yard line, where a Chicago player picks up the ball and runs it in. What would you rule?

    a. Touchdown for the Bears.
    b. Touchback for the Vikings.
    c. Safety against the Vikings.
    d. Bears' ball on the Vikings' 2-yard line.

10. All-star aberration

In a Pro Bowl game, the NFC has the ball on the AFC's 30-yard line. The NFC quarterback drops back to pass and throws a beauty to his wide receiver, who catches it on the AFC's 4-yard line. When the wide receiver reaches the 3, one of the AFC defenders reaches up, grabs him by the face mask, and flips him forward. The receiver hits the ground on the 2 but drops the ball before he lands. The ball rolls into the end zone and over the end line. How would you call it?

a. Touchdown for the NFC.
b. Touchdown for the NFC and a 15-yard penalty against the AFC on the next kickoff.
c. NFC's ball, first down on the AFC's 1-yard line.
d. NFC's ball, first down on the AFC's 2-yard line.

11. High rate of exchange

On the opening kickoff of a game between Los Angeles and Atlanta, the Rams' return man catches the ball on his own 10-yard line and runs toward his left on a criss-cross pattern. He hands the ball forward to a teammate at his 15-yard line. At the 16, the new ball carrier is tackled and fumbles. An Atlanta defender recovers at the 16, then runs the ball into the Rams' end zone. How would you rule it?

    a. Touchdown for Atlanta.
    b. Atlanta's ball, first and 10 from the Rams' 16.
    c. Rams' ball, first and 10 from their 16.
    d. Rams' ball, first and 10 from their 10.

12. Variations on a theme of rejection

On fourth down with the ball on the 50-yard line, Buffalo's punter takes the snap at his own 38. A Los Angeles lineman breaks through and blocks the punt. The ball rolls to the Bills' 30, with one Ram and one Bill chasing it. The Ram uses his hands to push the Bill out of the way, then picks up the ball and runs it into Buffalo's end zone. How would you rule it?

a. Touchdown for Los Angeles.
b. Ram's ball, first and 10 from Buffalo's 30.
c. Bills' ball, first and 10 from their 35.
d. Bills' ball, first and 10 from their 45.

13. Zero for artistry

On second and 10 from his own 10-yard line, the Saints' quarterback takes the snap and rolls out to his right. He crosses the line of scrimmage and goes to the 11, where he throws a forward pass to his wide receiver. As the receiver reaches up for the ball at his 30-yard line, a Rams defensive back pushes him away from the ball, intercepts it, and runs into New Orleans's end zone. What would you rule?

   a. Defensive pass interference, Saints' ball at their 30.
   b. Touchdown for Los Angeles.
   c. Saints' ball, third and 14 from their 6.
   d. Re-play the down, because both teams fouled on the play.

14. Guess the location

Chicago kicks off to Indianapolis. The ball goes 15 yards downfield to the 50. A strong wind then catches the ball in midair and blows it back toward Chicago's 30-yard line. One of the Chicago players falls on it at the 30. Keep in mind that the ball has traveled 15 yards forward before being blown back. What would you rule?

    a. Chicago's ball, first and 10 from its 30.
    b. Re-kick, with a five-yard penalty against Chicago for a short free kick.
    c. Indianapolis's ball, first and 10 from Chicago's 30.
    d. Indianapolis's ball, first and 10 from the 50.

15. Improvisational drama

The Green Bay Packers are in a punting situation (fourth and 10) at their own 30-yard line. The Packers' center snaps the ball to the punter, but the punt is partially blocked by a Bears linebacker. The ball goes two yards beyond the line of scrimmage to the Packers' 32, where it touches one of the Packers' players. It then rebounds behind the line of scrimmage, and the punter picks it up at his 25. He then throws a pass to his wide receiver, who catches it at the Packers' 35 and runs 65 yards, into the Bears' end zone. The fans at Lambeau Field go crazy. Cool-headed as ever, how do you rule it?

a. Touchdown for Green Bay.
b. Green Bay's ball, first and 10 from its 25.
c. Chicago's ball, first and 10 from Green Bay's 25.
d. Chicago's ball, first and 10 from Green Bay's 32.

16. Changing roles in mid-career

With fourth down and goal to go at Cincinnati's 2-yard line, Cleveland lines up for a field goal attempt. The holder kneels at the Bengals' 9, with the kicker ready to move forward. The snap from center is high, and the ball goes off the holder's hands. It rolls to Cincinnati's 12, where the kicker picks it up and throws a legal forward pass to his tight end, who catches it at the line of scrimmage and runs into the end zone. What do you rule?

a. Touchdown for Cleveland.
b. Touchback.
c. Cincinnati's ball, first and 10 from its 9.
d. Cincinnati's ball, first and 10 from its 12.

17. Meanwhile, in another part of our nation's capital . . .

St. Louis has the ball on the Washington 45-yard line, third down and 15. The Cardinals' quarterback fakes a pass and hands the ball to his running back on a draw play. The back runs to the Redskins' 30, where he fumbles and a Redskin recovers. During the running back's progress, a Washington defensive back holds a St. Louis wide receiver at the Redskins' 40. How do you rule it?

    a. Redskins' ball, first and 10 at their own 15 (after a 15-yard penalty from where the ball was recovered).

    b. Cardinals' ball, first and 10 at the Redskins' 40 (after a five-yard penalty for defensive holding, measured from the spot of the previous snap).

    c. Cardinals' ball, first and 10 at the Redskins' 35 (after a five-yard penalty for defensive holding from the spot of the foul).

    d. Cardinals' ball, first and 10 at the Redskins' 15 (after a 15-yard penalty against the Redskins, measured from the spot of the fumble and the ball's being returned to the Cardinals).

18. Funny, he was here just a minute ago

Cleveland faces second down and 10 on Houston's 40-yard line. A Cleveland running back goes downfield, close to the sideline, trying to get open for a pass. A Houston linebacker legally chucks him out of bounds. The running back immediately comes back onto the field of play and jumps to try to catch a perfectly thrown pass. With the ball in the air, the linebacker pushes the running back again, but the latter makes the catch anyway. He runs the ball into Houston's end zone. How do you rule it?

a. Touchdown for Cleveland.
b. Cleveland's ball, second and 10 at Houston's 40.
c. Cleveland's ball, third and 10 at Houston's 40.
d. Cleveland's ball, third and 25 at its 45.

19. Something extra times two

New Orleans has the ball on its own 40-yard line. It is third down and 10. A New Orleans running back is tackled at his 36, where he fumbles, then bats the loose ball forward from his 36 to his 42. There, a New Orleans teammate recovers the ball. New Orleans was offside. How do you rule it?

a. New Orleans's ball, third and 29 on its 21.
b. New Orleans's ball, fourth and 8 from its 42.
c. New Orleans's ball, third and 15 from its 35.
d. New Orleans's ball, third and 25 from its 25 (after a 15-yard penalty from the spot of the previous snap).

20. Volleying deep

San Diego has third down and 18 from its 4-yard line. The Chargers' quarterback throws a forward pass from his end zone. The ball is batted back by a Houston linebacker. It goes right back into the quarterback's hands. He is standing in the end zone. He then flips the ball forward to one of his running backs, who also is in the end zone. The running back is tackled immediately. He fumbles. The Houston linebacker who originally batted the ball now recovers it in the end zone. How do you rule it?

    a. San Diego's ball, fourth and 18 on its 4.
    b. San Diego's ball, fourth and 20 on its 2.
    c. Touchdown for Houston.
    d. Safety against San Diego.

21. Worth putting in the playbook?

The Los Angeles Rams' kicker attempts a field goal from the San Francisco 30-yard line, seven yards behind the line of scrimmage. The kick is wide. The ball touches a 49er as he tries to catch it in the end zone. It then rolls out to the 49ers' 3, where the Rams' tight end falls on it. What would you rule?

a. Rams' ball, first down at the 49ers' 30.
b. Touchback.
c. 49ers' ball, first and 10 from their 23.
d. 49ers' ball, first and 10 from their 30.

22. The ultimate dump-off

On third and 15 from his 4-yard line, the Indianapolis quarterback takes the snap from his center and drops back into the end zone to throw a forward pass. A Cincinnati defensive end crashes through and is about to tackle the quarterback, when he intentionally throws the ball down in front of himself while in the end zone. The defensive end falls on the ball in the end zone. How would you rule it?

  a. Safety.
  b. Touchdown.
  c. Colts' ball, fourth and 15 from their 4.
  d. Colts' ball, fourth and 17 from their 2.

23. Please hold all applause

On third down with the ball on Miami's 8-yard line, New England's quarterback takes the snap. He immediately throws a backward pass to his fullback, who can't quite catch the ball. The fullback juggles it as he is running forward, and the ball falls out of his hands on the 5-yard line. The fullback never had control of it. The ball rolls into Miami's end zone, where a Miami safety picks it up and runs the length of the field, into New England's end zone. How would you rule it?

a. Touchdown.
b. Touchback.
c. Safety.
d. Incomplete pass, fourth down for New England on Miami's 8-yard line.

24. Catch!

Washington's return man waits for a punt in his own end zone. He comes out of the end zone, catches the ball a foot or so in front of the goal line, and steps back into the end zone. He then flips the ball to the field judge covering the play. The field judge blows his whistle. What is the correct call?

    a. Touchback.
    b. Safety.
    c. Inadvertent whistle. Put the ball in play on the Washington 1-yard line.
    d. Re-play the entire play.

25. Don't look back

On fourth down, with the ball at New Orleans's 40-yard line, the Saints' punter stands with his hands outstretched, waiting to receive the snap from center. The ball sails over the punter's head and lands on the Saints' 20. The punter, meanwhile, has turned and is trying to recover the ball. However, a San Francisco defensive end pushes the punter from behind, moving him out of the way. The 49ers' defender then picks up the ball on New Orleans's 15-yard line and runs it into the Saints' end zone. How would you rule it?

a. Touchdown.
b. Clipping penalty against San Francisco, 15 yards from the spot of the snap. First down for New Orleans.
c. 49ers' ball, first down where the defensive end recovered the ball (the 15).
d. 49ers' ball, first down with a 15-yard penalty against the 49ers from the spot where the pushing took place.

26. Transition game

Denver kicks off to start the game. The Houston return man waits in his end zone. He tries to catch the ball there, but it slips through his hands. He bends over to pick up the ball in the end zone and accidentally kicks it out to his 10-yard line. A Denver player picks it up and runs it into Houston's end zone. Before he has crossed the goal line, one of his teammates holds a Houston player at the 6. How would you rule it?

a. Touchdown for Denver and a 15-yard penalty against Houston on the ensuing kickoff.
b. Denver's ball, first down on the Houston 10.
c. Denver's ball, first down on the Houston 21.
d. Safety against Houston for kicking a loose ball in its end zone.

27. Letting go

It is Denver's ball, second down and 20 from its 30. The Broncos' quarterback drops back and throws a forward pass. Just as the ball leaves his hand, a blitzing Dallas linebacker roughs the quarterback. Denver's wide receiver catches the ball at midfield and runs to the Dallas 40, where he is tackled and fumbles. Dallas recovers the ball on its own 35. How would you rule it?

a. Denver's ball, first down at its 45, after penalizing Dallas 15 yards from the spot of the previous snap.

b. Denver's ball, first down at Dallas's 40.

c. Denver's ball, first down at Dallas's 25, after penalizing Dallas 15 yards from the spot of the fumble.

d. Dallas's ball, first down from its 15-yard line, after penalizing the Cowboys 15 yards from where they recovered.

28. Coming to grips

Minnesota faces second down on Indianapolis's 40-yard line. The Vikings' quarterback drops back to pass. One of the Colts' defensive tackles comes in from the "blind side" and tackles the quarterback, who drops the ball before he hits the ground. A Colts player picks up the ball at midfield and runs it into the Vikings' end zone. While the quarterback was dropping back to pass, a Colts linebacker held a Vikings wide receiver on the Colts' 30-yard line. How would you rule it?

- a. Touchdown, holding penalty against Indianapolis on the ensuing kickoff.
- b. Minnesota's ball, first down on the Colts' 25.
- b. Minnesota's ball, first down on the Colts' 30.
- d. Minnesota's ball, first down on the Colts' 35.

29. Homemade option play

St. Louis has the ball, fourth down and two yards to go at Pittsburgh's 8-yard line. St. Louis lines up for a field goal. The snap is high and goes off the hands of the holder, who is kneeling at Pittsburgh's 15. The kicker picks up the ball and tries to run for a first down or a touchdown. He runs to Pittsburgh's 7 and spots an eligible receiver in the end zone. He throws the ball from the 7. One of the Pittsburgh defenders pushes the eligible receiver from behind as he tries to catch the ball. The ball hits the goal post, and the receiver catches it in the end zone before it hits the ground. What would you rule?

a. Touchback for Pittsburgh.
b. St. Louis's ball, first down on Pittsburgh's 1-yard line.
c. Touchdown for St. Louis.
d. Pittsburgh's ball, first down on its 12.

30. The opposite of "Captain, may I?"

Minnesota faces second down on Los Angeles's 20-yard line. The Vikings' quarterback throws a pass to his wide receiver, but a Rams' defensive back intercepts on his 2-yard line, with his back to his own goal line. The backward momentum carries him one step, then a second step, backward. He is just inside the goal line when he is tackled and downed. How would you rule it?

    a. Safety against the Rams.
    b. Touchback for the Rams, first down on their 20.
    c. Rams' ball, first down on their 2.
    d. Rams' ball, first down on their 1.

NFL Lists

If you're a fan of cubbyholes and compartments, you'll probably wonder why we've omitted categories such as "left-footed outside linebackers of the NFC East." Our apologies. And while we're cross-referencing our archives for more related irrelevance, you'll have to satisfy yourself with the groups that appear here. It goes without saying that each sub-heading is quiz bait in itself. So why did we say it?

1. Charter members

The original American Football League franchises of 1960.

Boston Patriots
Buffalo Bills
Dallas Texans
Denver Broncos
Houston Oilers
Los Angeles Chargers
New York *Titans*
Oakland Raiders

2. Ten times the number from Olive Branch, Mississippi

Ten recent NFL players from Shreveport, Louisiana:
1. Terry Bradshaw
2. Joe Ferguson
3. Isaac Hagins
4. Jim Harlan
5. Bo Harris
6. Ezra Johnson
7. Gary Johnson
8. Tom Owen
9. Robert Pennywell
10. Charles Philyaw

3. Next of kin

Brothers who have played in the NFL:

1. Ted, Lou, and Alex Karras
2. Bill, Rich, and Ron Saul
3. Phil and Merlin Olsen
4. Ed and Dick Modzelewski
5. Tody and Bubba Smith
6. Marvin and Gene Upshaw
7. Art and Benny Malone
8. Steve and Nick Mike-Mayer
9. Bob and Dick Anderson
10. Dewey and Lee Roy Selmon
11. Chuck Muncie and Nelson Munsey
12. Lyle and Glenn Blackwood
13. Lin, Walt, and Jim Houston

4. Lead oxen

All-Time Top 10 Rushers:

PLAYER	YEARS	ATT.	YARDS	AVG.	LONG	TD
Walter Payton	10	3,047	13,309	4.4	76	89
Jim Brown	9	2,359	12,312	5.2	80	106
Franco Harris	13	2,949	12,120	4.1	75	91
O.J. Simpson	11	2,404	11,236	4.7	94	61
John Riggins	13	2,740	10,675	3.9	66	96
Tony Dorsett	8	2,136	9,525	4.5	99	69
Earl Campbell	7	2,029	8,764	4.3	81	73
Jim Taylor	10	1,941	8,597	4.4	84	83
Joe Perry	14	1,737	8,378	4.8	78	53
Larry Csonka	11	1,891	8,081	4.3	54	64

Tommy Prothro, director of player personnel for the Cleveland Browns, was hit on the head by a foul ball while watching a baseball game at Portland's Multnomah Stadium. The batter at the time was his father, "Doc" Prothro, who played major league ball with the Washington Senators, Boston Red Sox, and Cincinnati Reds and later managed the Philadelphia Phillies.

5. On the Wing

All-Time Top 10 Passers:*

Player	Years	Att.	Comp.	Pct. Comp.	Yards	TD	Pct. TD	Int.	Pct. Int.	Avg. Gain	Rating
Joe Montana	6	2,077	1,324	63.7	15,609	106	5.1	54	2.6	7.52	92.7
Roger Staubach	11	2,958	1,685	57.0	22,700	153	5.2	109	3.7	7.67	83.4
Danny White	9	1,943	1,155	59.4	14,754	109	5.6	90	4.6	7.59	82.7
Sonny Jurgensen	18	4,262	2,433	57.1	32,224	255	6.0	189	4.4	7.56	82.6
Len Dawson	19	3,741	2,136	57.1	28,711	239	6.4	183	4.9	7.67	82.6
Ken Anderson	14	4,420	2,627	59.4	32,497	194	4.4	158	3.6	7.35	82.0
Dan Fouts	12	4,380	2,585	59.0	33,854	201	4.6	185	4.2	7.73	81.2
Bart Starr	16	3,149	1,808	57.4	24,718	152	4.8	138	4.4	7.85	80.5
Fran Tarkenton	18	6,467	3,686	57.0	47,003	342	5.3	266	4.1	7.27	80.4
Joe Theismann	11	3,301	1,877	56.9	23,432	152	4.6	132	4.0	7.10	79.0

*1,500 or more attempts. The passing ratings are based on performance standards established for completion percentage, interception percentage, touchdown percentage, and average gain. Passers are allocated points according to how their marks compare with those standards.

6. Highly receptive

All-Time Top 10 Pass Receivers:

Player	Yrs.	No.	Yds.	Avg.	Long	TD
Charlie Joiner	16	657	10,774	16.4	87	56
Charley Taylor	13	649	9,110	14.0	88	79
Don Maynard	15	633	11,834	18.7	87	88
Raymond Berry	13	631	9,275	14.7	70	68
Harold Carmichael	13	589	8,978	15.2	85	79
Fred Biletnikoff	14	589	8,974	15.2	82	76
Harold Jackson	16	579	10,372	17.9	79	76
Lionel Taylor	10	567	7,195	12.7	80	45
Steve Laugent	9	545	8,772	16.1	74	72
Lance Alworth	11	542	10,266	18.9	85	85

7. Prolific

All-Time Top 10 Scorers:

Player	Years	TD	FG	PAT	TP
George Blanda	26	9	335	943	2,002
Jan Stenerud	18	0	358	539	1,613
Jim Turner	16	1	304	521	1,439
Jim Bakken	17	0	282	534	1,380
Fred Cox	15	0	282	519	1,365
Lou Groza	17	1	234	641	1,349
Gino Cappelletti*	11	42	176	350	1,130
Mark Moseley	14	0	266	426	1,224
Don Cockroft	13	0	216	432	1,080
Garo Yepremian	14	0	210	444	1,074

*Cappelletti's total includes four two-point conversions

8. Familiar with paydirt

All-Time Top 10 Touchdown Scorers:

Player	Years	Rush	Pass Rec.	Returns	Total TD
Jim Brown	9	106	20	0	126
Lenny Moore	12	63	48	2	113
John Riggins	12	96	12	0	108
Don Hutson	11	3	99	3	105
Franco Harris	12	91	9	0	100
Walter Payton	10	89	9	0	98
Jim Taylor	10	83	10	0	93
Bobby Mitchell	11	18	65	8	91
Leroy Kelly	10	74	13	3	90
Charley Taylor	13	11	79	0	90

Compton (California) Junior College listed the following former NFL players as coaches of its football teams in the 1970s: head coach Art Perkins and assistants Marlin Briscoe, Henry Dyer, Essex Johnson, Deacon Jones, and Joe Sweet. Also stopping by, on occasion, were Lawrence McCutcheon and Ron Jessie of the Los Angeles Rams.

9. Paragons of patience

Nineteen men who played all ten seasons of the American Football League, 1960–69:

1. George Blanda
2. Billy Cannon
3. Gino Cappelletti
4. Larry Grantham
5. Wayne Hawkins
6. Jim (Earthquake) Hunt
7. Harry Jacobs
8. Jack Kemp
9. Paul Lowe
10. Jacky Lee
11. Bill Mathis
12. Paul Maguire
13. Don Maynard
14. Ron Mix
15. Jim Otto
16. Babe Parilli
17. Johnny Robinson
18. Paul Rochester
19. Ernie Wright

10. Time capsule

All-AFL Team:

Offense

Fred Arbanas, TE
Ron Mix, T
Billy Shaw, G
Jim Otto, C
Ed Budde, G
Jim Tyrer, T
Lance Alworth, WR
Don Maynard, WR
Joe Namath, QB
Paul Lowe, RB
Clem Daniels, RB
George Blanda, K

Defense

Jerry Mays, DE
Tom Sestak, DT
Houston Antwine, DT
Gerry Philbin, DE
George Webster, LB
Nick Buoniconti, LB
Bobby Bell, LB
Willie Brown, CB
Dave Grayson, CB
Johnny Robinson, S
George Saimes, S
Jerrel Wilson, P

11. So what became of 33?

Number 32 was considered the number of prominent running backs (e.g., Jim Brown, O.J. Simpson, Franco Harris) for many years. Today's stars wear number 34:

Earl Campbell, Saints
Walter Abercrombie, Steelers
Walter Payton, Bears
Greg Pruitt, Raiders
Rickey Young, Vikings

12. The "farm system"

Top 10 colleges sending players into the NFL:

1. USC — 44
2. Penn State — 41
3. UCLA — 29
4. Texas — 28
5. Arizona State — 27
6. Michigan State — 27
7. Pittsburgh — 26
8. Alabama — 25
9. Notre Dame — 22
10. Nebraska — 21
11. Oklahoma — 21

In 1960, the offensive backfield for Taft High School in Cincinnati was Al Nelson, quarterback, and Walter Johnson, Carl Ward, and Cid Edwards, running backs. Nelson played safety for the Philadelphia Eagles (1965–1973); Johnson played defensive tackle for the Cleveland Browns (1965–1976); Ward was a safety with Cleveland (1967–68) and New Orleans (1969); and Edwards was a running back with St. Louis (1968–1971), San Diego (1972–74), and Chicago (1975).

*From 1980 veteran rosters

13. Indoor-outdoor specialists

Ten NFL players who also played professional basketball:

Player, NFL Team	Basketball Team and First Year
1. Bud Grant, Eagles	Minneapolis Lakers, 1950–51
2. Connie Mack Berry, Bears	Oshkosh All-Stars, 1940–41
3. Otto Graham, Browns	Rochester Royals, 1946–47
4. Dick Evans, Packers	Sheboygan Redskins, 1941–42
5. Ted Fritsch, Packers	Oshkosh All-Stars, 1945–46
6. Len Ford, Browns	Dayton Rens, 1949–50
7. Otto Schnellbacher, Giants	St. Louis Bombers, 1948–49
8. Bob Shaw, Rams	Youngstown Bears, 1945–46
9. Ron Widby, Cowboys	New Orleans Buccaneers, 1967–68
10. Lonnie Wright, Broncos	Denver Rockets, 1967–68

14. How long does it take?

For an NFL team to complete summer training camp	45 days
To complete an NFL game	3 hours
For an NFL team to complete a practice session	1½ hours
For a wide receiver to cover 40 yards	4.4 seconds
For a 250 pound lineman to cover 40 yards ..	5.1 seconds
For a good punt to stay in the air (hang time)	5.0 seconds
To convert an NFL stadium from baseball to football	8 hours
For a quarterback to drop back and set up to pass	2.3 seconds
For the average NFL player to complete his career	4.3 years

15. NFL Olympians

PLAYER	YEAR	EVENT	MEDAL
Jim Thorpe	1912	decathlon,	gold
		pentathlon	gold
Harold (Brick) Muller	1920	high jump	silver
Sol Butler	1920	long jump	none
Jim Bausch	1932	decathlon	gold
Pete Mehringer	1932	wrestling (light heavy-weight)	gold
Jack Torrance	1936	shot put	none
Clyde (Smackover) Scott	1948	110-meter hurdles	silver
Ollie Matson	1952	400 meters, 1,600 meter relay	bronze, silver

Milt Campbell	1952,	decathlon	silver,
	1956	decathlon	gold
Glenn Davis	1956,	intermediate hurdles,	gold
	1960	intermediate hurdles	gold
		1,600 meter relay	gold
Bo Roberson	1960	long jump	silver
Ray Norton	1960	100 meters,	none
		200 meters,	none,
		400 meter relay	gold
Frank Budd	1960	100 meters	none
Henry Carr	1964	200 meters,	gold
		1,600 meter relay	gold,
Bob Hayes	1964	100 meters,	gold
		400 meter relay	gold,
Jim Hines	1968	100 meters,	gold
		400 meter relay	gold
Tommie Smith	1968	200 meters	gold
Larry Burton	1972	200 meters	none
Gerald Tinker	1972	400 meter relay	gold
James Owens	1976	110 meter high hurdles	none
Johnny (Lam) Jones	1976	100 meters	none,
		400 meter relay	gold
Michael Carter	1984	shotput	silver
Ron Brown	1984	400 meter relay	gold

16. Fixtures

Top 11 active players with most games played:

When the NFL and the All-America Football Conference merged for the 1950 season, a showdown game between Philadelphia and Cleveland was scheduled on the Saturday night before the regular Sunday opening for the rest of the league. The Eagles were two-time champions of the NFL. The Browns had won the AAFC title all four years of that league's existence. The Browns won the game 35–10, but Eagles coach Earle (Greasy) Neale was quoted as calling the Browns "a basketball team that can only pass." In the return match on December 3, 1950, the Browns did not throw a single pass. They beat the Eagles 13–7.

17. Still Churning

Top 10 Active Rushers:

Player, Team	Years	Att.	Yards	Avg.	TDs
Walter Payton, Chicago	10	3,047	13,309	4.4	89
John Riggins, Washington	13	2,740	10,675	3.9	96
Tony Dorsett, Dallas	8	2,136	9,525	4.5	59
Earl Campbell, New Orleans	7	2,029	8,764	4.3	73
Otis Anderson, St. Louis	6	1,690	7,364	4.4	40
Chuck Muncie, San Diego	9	1,561	6,702	4.3	71
Mike Pruitt, Cleveland	9	1,593	6,540	4.1	47
Wilbert Montgomery, Philadelphia	8	1,465	6,538	4.5	45
William Andrews, Falcons	5	1,263	5,772	4.6	29
Greg Pruitt, L.A. Raiders	12	1,196	5,672	4.7	27

18. Pitch Till You Win

Top 10 Active Passers:

Player, Team	Years	Att.	Comp.	Pct. Comp.	Yards	TD	Pct. TD	Int.	Pct. Int.	Avg. Gain	Rating
Joe Montana, S.F.	6	2,077	1,324	63.7	15,609	106	5.1	54	2.6	7.52	92.7
Neil Lomax, St. L.	4	1,355	782	57.7	10,192	61	4.5	43	3.2	7.52	83.3
Danny White, Dallas	9	1,943	1,155	59.4	14,754	109	5.6	90	4.6	7.59	82.7
Ken Anderson, Cin.	14	4,420	2,627	59.4	32,497	194	4.4	158	3.6	7.35	82.0
Dan Fouts, S.D.	12	4,380	2,585	59.0	33,854	201	4.6	185	4.2	7.73	81.2
Joe Theismann, Wash.	11	3,301	1,877	56.9	23,432	152	4.6	132	4.0	7.10	79.0
Bill Kenney, K.C.	5	1,397	776	55.5	10,163	60	4.3	52	3.7	7.27	77.5
Steve Bartkowski, Atl.	10	3,219	1,802	56.0	22,732	149	4.6	140	4.3	7.06	75.5
Vince Ferragamo, Rams	7	1,288	730	56.7	9,376	70	5.4	71	5.5	7.28	74.8
Gary Danielson, Det.	9	1,684	952	56.5	11,885	69	4.1	71	4.2	7.06	74.7

19. Good Hands People

Top 10 Active Pass Receivers:

Player, Team	Years	No.	Yards	Avg.	TDs
Charlie Joiner, San Diego	16	657	10,774	16.4	56
Steve Largent, Seattle	9	545	8,772	16.1	72
Cliff Branch, L.A. Raiders	13	501	8,685	17.3	67
Ozzie Newsome, Cleveland	7	440	5,570	12.7	34
Nat Moore, Miami	11	421	6,414	15.2	60
Isaac Curtis, Cincinnati	12	416	7,101	17.1	53
Pat Tilley, St. Louis	9	416	6,228	15.0	31
Tony Galbreath, N.Y. Giants	9	401	3,223	8.0	8
Kellen Winslow, San Diego	6	399	5,176	13.0	37
James Lofton, Green Bay	7	397	7,663	19.3	41

20. Mostly Just for Kicks

Top 10 Active Scorers:

Player, Team	Years	TD	XP	XPA	FG	FGA	Points
Jan Stenerud, Minnesota	18	0	539	558	358	532	1,613
Mark Moseley, Washington	14	0	426	452	266	404	1,224
Ray Wersching, San Fran.	12	0	319	336	171	256	832
Pat Leahy, N.Y. Jets	11	0	306	329	158	239	780
Rafael Septien, Dallas	8	0	335	347	146	207	773
Chris Bahr, L.A. Raiders	9	0	321	344	146	235	759
Rolf Benirschke, San Diego	8	0	287	311	130	183	677
John Riggins, Washington	13	108	0	0	0	0	648
Bob Thomas, Chicago	10	0	248	270	133	210	647
Walter Payton, Chicago	10	98	0	0	0	0	588

The AFL adopted the two-point conversion option for its first season of play in 1960. The point value was two if successfully converted by a pass or running play, one if kicked in the conventional manner.

21. Not just a nickname

In 1922 and 1923, Marion, Ohio, had an NFL franchise that was sponsored by the Oorang Airedale Kennels. The team, known as the Oorang Indians and coached by Jim Thorpe, was made up of native Americans. A partial list of the players:

1. Arowhead
2. Black Bear
3. Deerslayer
4. Xavier Downwind
5. Laughing Gas
6. Joe Little Twig
7. Red Fang
8. Stilwell Sanooke
9. Baptiste Thunder
10. Wrinkle Meat
11. Deadeye
12. Lone Wolf

22. Papa Bear says

George Halas's list of the twelve best quarterbacks he ever saw:

1. Sid Luckman: " 'Mr. Quarterback' . . . the first of the modern quarterbacks . . . set the pattern for man-in-motion T-formation."
2. Sammy Baugh: "Fired a bullet-like pass with the flick of his wrist . . . tremendous player to watch . . . poised at all times."
3. Otto Graham: "Team leader, unflinching when the going got tough . . . knew how to make a play work."
4. Bobby Layne: "Fiery, skilled quarterback . . . great field general . . . dominant figure on the field, team leader."
5. Bart Starr: "Cool and calculating . . . tremendous respect from teammates . . . a fine field general with a great arm."
6. Fran Tarkenton: "The first scrambling quarterback . . . his records speak for his durability and talent."
7. Johnny Unitas: "Great poise and leadership . . . a pressure player with full confidence of team . . . outstanding passer with great knowledge of the game."
8. Norm Van Brocklin: "Highly emotional, skilled leader . . . strong arm, great timing on long or short passes."
9. Bob Waterfield: "Superb, confident quarterback . . . versatile as runner, passer, punter, placekicker, and defender . . . inspiring leader."
10. Terry Bradshaw: "An outstanding field general . . . strong and accurate passer . . . great physical equipment . . . a winner."
11. Roger Staubach: "Inspirational leader . . . very cool in pressure situations . . . dangerous from anywhere, at anytime."
12. Ken Stabler: "Outstanding late in the game, when points are needed . . . thrives in clutch situations."

23. Now look, Dean. . . .

The 11 current NFL officials who are ex-NFL players:

1. Ron Botchan, Chargers, Oilers
2. Royal Cathcart, 49ers
3. Pat Harder, Cardinals, Lions
4. Pat Knight, Giants
5. Dean Look, Jets
6. Leo Miles, Giants
7. Carver Shannon, Rams
8. Pete Liske, Browns, Broncos, Jets, Eagles
9. Fred Wyant, Redskins
10. Merrill Douglas, Bears, Cowboys, Eagles
11. Gary Lane, Browns, Giants

24. Nice going, junior

Five NFL players who won the Heisman Trophy as college juniors:

1. Doak Walker, Southern Methodist, 1948—Lions
2. Vic Janowicz, Ohio State, 1950—Redskins
3. Roger Staubach, Navy, 1963—Cowboys
4. Archie Griffin, Ohio State, 1974—Bengals
5. Billy Sims, Oklahoma, 1978—Lions

Former NFL Commissioner Bert Bell, under whose direction the League reached new stability and acceptance, suffered a fatal heart attack while attending the Philadelphia Eagles-Pittsburgh Steelers game at Franklin Field, October 11, 1959. Bell had been associated with both teams as a coach and executive prior to taking over as Commissioner in 1946.

25. Laugh all you want ...

Twelve men who have played in the NFL:

1. June Jones
2. Margene Adkins
3. Gail Cogdill
4. Blenda Gay
5. Fair Hooker
6. Dolly King
7. Blanche Martin
8. Kay McFarland
9. Julie Rykovich
10. Bev Wallace
11. Faye Wilson
12. Tillie Manton

26. And they're all close friends of Howard Cosell

Ivy Leaguers in the NFL:

1. Pat McInally, P, Bengals, Harvard
2. Reggie Williams, LB, Bengals, Dartmouth
3. John Spagnola, TE, Eagles, Yale
4. Gary Fencik, S, Bears, Yale
5. George Starke, T, Redskins, Columbia
6. Kenny Hill, S, Raiders, Yale
7. Nick Lowrey, K., Chiefs, Dartmouth
8. Florian Kempf, K, Oilers, Pennsylvania
9. Joe Dufek, QB, Bills, Yale
10. Joe Pellegrini, C, Jets, Harvard
11. John Woodring, LB, Jets, Brown
12. Bob Holly, QB, Eagles, Princeton
13. Jeff Rohrer, LB, Cowboys, Yale
14. Jeff Kemp, QB, Rams, Dartmouth
15. Steve Jordan, TE, Vikings, Brown
16. John Witkowski, QB, Lions, Columbia

27. Where have you gone, Haywood Sullivan?

Major league baseball players drafted by the NFL:

	PLAYER	COLLEGE	NFL TEAM	ROUND	YR.
1.	Sam Chapman	California	Redskins	2	1938
2.	George (Snuffy) Stirnweiss	N. Carolina	Chicago Cardinals	2	1940
3.	Alvin Dark	LSU	Eagles	2	1945
4.	Walt Dropo	Connecticut	Bears	9	1946
5.	Lloyd Merriman	Stanford	Chicago Cardinals	3	1947
6.	Bill Renna	Santa Clara	Rams	12	1949

7.	Haywood Sullivan	Florida	Chicago Cardinals	25	1953
8.	Norm Cash	Sul Ross State	Bears	13	1955
9.	Jake Gibbs	Mississippi	Browns	9	1961
10.	Merv Rettenmund	Ball State	Cowboys	19	1965
11.	Dave Winfield	Minnesota	Vikings	17	1973

28. Global

Eleven foreign-born NFL players:

1. Rick Berns, RB, Raiders—Okinawa, Japan
2. Mosi Tatupu, RB, Patriots—Pago Pago, Samoa
3. Jack Thompson, QB, Buccaneers—American Samoa
4. Allan Kennedy, T, 49ers—Vancouver, Canada
5. Luis Sharpe, T, Cardinals—Havana, Cuba
6. Craig Bingham, LB, Steelers—Kingston, Jamaica
7. Tunch Ilkin, T, Steelers—Istanbul, Turkey
8. Guy Bingham, C, Jets—Koizumi Guama Ken, Japan
9. Justin Cross, T, Bills—Montreal, Canada
10. Jeff Nixon, S, Bills—Forstein Feldbruch, Germany
11. John Sinnott, T, Colts—Wexford, Ireland

For a brief time during the offseason in 1950 the NFL was known as the "National-American Football League. This was after the merger of the NFL and the All-America Football Conference, which saw the Baltimore Colts, Cleveland Browns, and San Francisco 49ers join the established league from the defunct AAFC.

29. Coming at it from a different angle

Foreign-born kickers in the NFL:

1. Nick Lowery, Chiefs—Munich, Germany
2. Gary Anderson, Stellers—Parys, Orange Free State, South Africa
3. Uwe von Schamann, Dolphins—West Berlin, Germany
4. Raul Allegre, Colts—Torreon Coagula, Mexico
5. Rafael Septien, Cowboys—Mexico City, Mexico
6. Neil O'Donoghue, Cardinals—Dublin, Ireland
7. Morten Andersen, Saints—Struer, Denmark
8. Ray Wersching, 49ers—Monsdee, Austria
9. Mick Luckhurst, Falcons—Redbourn, England
10. Ed Murray, Lions—Halifax (Nova Scotia), Canada

30. Blocks and their respective chips

Twelve NFL father/son combinations:

1. Tony and Mike Adamle
2. Harold and Hal Bradley
3. Jim and Walker Gillette
4. John and Jack Gregory
5. Herb and John and Charley Hannah
6. Dub and Bert Jones
7. George and Jim Kiick
8. Bill and Pete Lazetich
9. Gil and Jim Steinke
10. Wilford (Whizzer) and Danny White
11. Ray and Mike Renfro
12. Jack and Jeff Kemp

31. Versatile

Ten players from other sports drafted by the NFL:

PLAYER	COLLEGE	N.F.L. TEAM	ROUND	YR.	SPORT
1. Mel Patton	USC	Giants	21	1946	track
2. K. C. Jones	San Francisco	Rams	30	1955	basketball
3. Johnny Kerr	Illinois	49ers	26	1955	basketball
4. Dave Sime	Duke	Lions	29	1959	track
5. Randy Matson	Texas A&M	Falcons	5	1967	track
6. Dave Lattin	Texas Western	Chiefs	17	1967	basketball
7. Jimmy Walker	Providence	Saints	17	1967	basketball
8. Joe Cowan	Johns Hopkins	Colts	12	1969	lacrosse
9. Willie Davenport	Southern U.	Saints	12	1970	track
10. Bart Buetow	Minnesota	Vikings	3	1972	hockey

32. Back to haunt them

Eleven quarterbacks who won championships after being traded or waived:

1. George Blanda, from Chicago Bears to Houston Oilers
2. Len Dawson, Cleveland Browns to Kansas City Chiefs
3. Jack Kemp, San Diego Chargers to Buffalo Bills
4. Bobby Layne, New York Bulldogs to Detroit Lions
5. Earl Morrall, New York Giants to Baltimore Colts
6. Bill Nelsen, Pittsburgh Steelers to Cleveland Browns
7. Frank Ryan, Los Angeles Rams to Cleveland Browns
8. Fran Tarkenton, New York Giants to Minnesota Vikings
9. Y.A. Tittle, San Francisco 49ers to New York Giants
10. Norm Van Brocklin, Los Angeles Rams to Philadelphia Eagles
11. Jim Plunkett, San Francisco 49ers to Oakland and Los Angeles Raiders

The last NFL team to switch to the T-formation was the Pittsburgh Steelers. After clinging to the single-wing years longer than the other teams, they made the changeover for the 1952 season.

33. Some do; some don't

The Heisman Trophy is awarded annually to what is termed "the most outstanding player in the country" in college football. For a variety of reasons, not all winners have gone on to play in the NFL.

Did

Davey O'Brien, quarterback, TCU 1938
Tom Harmon, halfback, Michigan..................1940
Bruce Smith, halfback, Minnesota..................1941
Frank Sinkwich, halfback, Georgia 1942
Angelo Bertelli, quarterback, Notre Dame 1943
Les Horvath, halfback, Ohio State 1944
Glenn Davis, halfback, Army 1946
Johnny Lujack, quarterback, Notre Dame............1947
Doak Walker, halfback, SMU 1948
Leon Hart, end, Notre Dame 1949
Vic Janowicz, halfback, Ohio State................1950
Billy Vessels, halfback, Oklahoma 1952
Johnny Lattner, halfback, Notre Dame 1953
Alan Ameche, fullback, Wisconsin 1954
Howard (Hopalong) Cassady, halfback, Ohio State 1955
Paul Hornung, quarterback, Notre Dame 1956
John David Crow, halfback, Texas A&M............1957
Billy Cannon, halfback, LSU.....................1959
Joe Bellino, halfback, Navy......................1960
Terry Baker, quarterback, Oregon State 1962
Roger Staubach, quarterback, Navy 1963
John Huarte, quarterback, Notre Dame 1964
Mike Garrett, halfback, USC.....................1965
Steve Spurrier, quarterback, Florida 1966
Gary Beban, quarterback, UCLA 1967
O.J. Simpson, running back, USC 1968

Steve Owens, running back, Oklahoma 1969
Jim Plunkett, quarterback, Stanford 1970
Pat Sullivan, quarterback, Auburn 1971
Johnny Rodgers, running back, Nebraska 1972
John Cappelletti, running back, Penn State 1973
Archie Griffin, running back, Ohio State 1974
Archie Griffin, running back, Ohio State 1975
Tony Dorsett, running back, Pittsburgh 1976
Earl Campbell, running back, Texas 1977
Billy Sims, running back, Oklahoma 1978
Charles White, running back, USC 1979
George Rogers, running back, South Carolina 1980
Marcus Allen, running back, USC 1981

Did Not

Jay Berwanger, halfback, Chicago 1935
Larry Kelley, end, Yale 1936
Clint Frank, halfback, Yale 1937
Nile Kinnick, halfback, Iowa 1939
Felix (Doc) Blanchard, fullback, Army 1945
Dick Kazmaier, halfback, Princeton 1951
Pete Dawkins, halfback, Army 1958
Ernie Davis, halfback, Syracuse 1961
Herschel Walker, running back, Georgia 1982
Mike Rozier, running back, Nebraska 1983
Doug Flutie, quarterback, Boston College 1984

34. The University of Coaching

Sixteen NFL coaches from Miami University (Ohio):

1. Paul Brown — Bengals and Browns
2. Weeb Ewbank — Browns, Colts, and Jets
3. Howard Brinker — Browns and Bengals
4. John Brickels — Browns
5. Sid Gillman — Rams, Chargers, Oilers, Bears, and Eagles
6. Fritz Heisler — Browns
7. John McVay — Giants and 49ers
8. Bruce Beatty — Patriots and Lions
9. Clive Rush — Jets and Patriots
10. Doc Urich — Broncos, Bills, and Redskins
11. Bill Arnsparger — Dolphins, Colts, and Giants
12. Ken Meyer — Jets, Rams, 49ers, and Bears
13. Jack Faulkner — Rams, Broncos, Saints, Vikings, and Chargers
14. Ed Biles — Saints, Jets, and Oilers
15. Jerry Wampfler — Eagles, Bills, and Giants
16. Joe Galat — Giants

The relatively small Oxford, Ohio, school has sent Woody Hayes, Ara Parseghian, Colonel Earl (Red) Blaik, Bo Schembechler, John Pont, Paul Dietzel, Carmen Cozza, Bill Mallory, and Dick Crum to the college coaching ranks. Former Dodger manager Walt Alston also is a Miami man.

35. Not-so-ancient history

Cities that have had NFL franchises:

CITY	TEAM	FIRST YEAR IN NFL
1. Canton, Ohio	Bulldogs	1920
2. Columbus, Ohio	Panhandles	1920
3. Dayton, Ohio	Triangles	1920
4. Duluth, Minnesota	Eskimos	1926
5. Evansville, Indiana	Crimson Giants	1922
6. Hammond, Indiana	Pros	1920
7. Hartford, Connecticut	Blues	1926
8. Portsmouth, Ohio	Spartans	1930
9. Pottsville, Pennsylvania	Maroons	1925
10. Providence, Rhode Island	Steamrollers	1925
11. Racine, Wisconsin	Legions	1922
12. Rochester, New York	Jeffersons	1920

36. Not a prerequisite

Current NFL coaches who did and did not play in the NFL:

Did	Did Not
Dan Reeves, Broncos	John Mackovic, Chiefs
Tom Flores, Raiders	Don Coryell, Chargers
Sam Wyche, Bengals	Chuck Knox, Seahawks
Chuck Noll, Steelers	Hugh Campbell, Oilers
Kay Stephenson, Bills	Rod Dowhower, Colts
Don Shula, Dolphins	John Robinson, Rams
Joe Walton, Jets	Bum Phillips, Saints
Dan Henning, Falcons	Bill Walsh, 49ers
Mike Ditka, Bears	Leeman Bennett, Buccaneers
Forrest Gregg, Packers	Bill Parcells, Giants
Tom Landry, Cowboys	Jim Hanifan, Cardinals
Marion Campbell, Eagles	Joe Gibbs, Redskins
Bud Grant, Vikings	Darryl Rogers, Lions
Raymond Berry, Patriots	
Marty Schotlenheimer, Browns	

Playing like the archetypal "Paper Lions," the Detroit Lions went winless (0–11) in 1942, giving up 263 points while scoring only 38.

37. As an actor, he's a helluva football player

Some NFL players who have acted in motion pictures:

1. Sammy Baugh........King of the Texas Rangers
2. Jim Boeke..................North Dallas Forty
3. Ben Davidson.....................M*A*S*H
4. Brian Duncan....................Semi-Tough
5. Carl Eller.......................The Black Six
6. Fred Gehrke......................Easy Living
7. Frank Gifford................Darby's Rangers
8. Red Grange................One Minute to Play
9. Joe Greene................Pop Goes the Weasel
10. Tom Harmon..............Harmon of Michigan
11. Mike Henry.......................Tarzan '65
12. Elroy Hirsch.......................Crazylegs
13. Mike Lucci........................Paper Lion
14. Bruce Smith...............Smith of Minnesota
15. Bob Waterfield...................Triple Threat

38. What does it MEAN?

In 10 of 18 Super Bowls, the winning quarterback has worn number 12:

Game III—Joe Namath, New York Jets
Game VI—Roger Staubach, Dallas Cowboys
Game VII—Bob Griese, Miami Dolphins
Game VIII—Bob Griese, Miami Dolphins
Game IX—Terry Bradshaw, Pittsburgh Steelers
Game X—Terry Bradshaw, Pittsburgh Steelers
Game XI—Ken Stabler, Oakland Raiders
Game XII—Roger Staubach, Dallas Cowboys
Game XIII—Terry Bradshaw, Pittsburgh Steelers
Game XIV—Terry Bradshaw, Pittsburgh Steelers

39. Centurians

NFL head coaches who have won 100 or more games:

Coach	Team(s)	Yrs.	Regular Season Won	Lost	Tied	Pct.
George Halas	Chicago Bears	40	319	148	31	.672
Don Shula	Baltimore Colts, Miami Dolphins	22	227	82	6	.730
Tom Landry	Dallas Cowboys	25	223	126	6	.637
Earl (Curly) Lambeau	Green Bay Packers, Chicago Cardinals, Washington Redskins	33	231	133	23	.627
Paul Brown	Cleveland Browns, Cincinnati Bengals	21	166	100	6	.621
Bud Grant	Minnesota Vikings	17	151	87	5	.633
Steve Owen	New York Giants	23	151	100	17	.595
Chuck Noll	Pittsburgh Steelers	16	142	88	1	.617
Hank Stram	Kansas City Chiefs, New Orleans Saints	17	131	97	10	.571
Weeb Ewbank	Baltimore Colts, New York Jets	20	130	129	7	.502
Sid Gillman	Los Angeles Rams, San Diego Chargers, Houston Oilers	18	122	99	7	.550
George Allen	Los Angeles Rams, Washington Redskins	12	116	47	5	.705
Chuck Knox	Los Angeles Rams, Buffalo Bills, Seattle Seahawks	12	112	62	1	.643
Ray (Buddy) Parker	Chicago Cardinals, Detroit Lions, Pittsburgh Steelers	15	104	75	9	.577
John Madden	Oakland Raiders	10	103	32	7	.750
Don Coryell	St. Louis Cardinals, San Diego Chargers	12	102	68	1	.599

40. You can't get there from here

1984 AFC TRAINING CAMP SITES

Club	Site	Location
Buffalo	Fredonia State Univ.	Fredonia, N.Y.
Cincinnati	Wilmington Coll.	Wilmington, Ohio
Cleveland	Lakeland Comm. Coll.	Mentor, Ohio
Denver	Northern Colorado Coll.	Greeley, Colo.
Houston	Angelo State Univ.	San Angelo, Tex.
Indianapolis	Anderson Coll.	Anderson, Ind.
Kansas City	William Jewell Coll.	Liberty, Mo.
L.A. Raiders	El Rancho Motel	Santa Rosa, Calif.
Miami	St. Thomas of Villanova	Miami, Fla.
New England	Bryant Coll.	Smithfield, R.I.
New York Jets	Hofstra Univ.	Hempstead, N.Y.
Pittsburgh	St. Vincent Coll.	Latrobe, Pa.
San Diego	California-San Diego	La Jolla, Calif.
Seattle	East Washington Univ.	Cheney, Wash.

1984 NFC TRAINING CAMP SITES

Atlanta	Falcons Complex	Suwanee, Ga.
Chicago	Halas Hall	Lake Forest, Ill.
Dallas	California Lutheran	Thousand Oaks, Calif.
Detroit	Oakland Univ.	Rochester, Mich.
Green Bay	St. Norbert Coll.	West DePere, Wis.
L.A. Rams	Cal. State-Fullerton	Fullerton, Calif.
Minnesota	Mankato State Univ.	Mankato, Minn.
New Orleans	Dodgertown	Vero Beach, Fla.
N.Y. Giants	Pace Univ.	Pleasantville, N.Y.
Philadelphia	West Chester State	West Chester, Pa.
St. Louis	Eastern Illinois Univ.	Charleston, Ill.
San Francisco	Sierra Community Coll.	Rocklin, Calif.
Tampa Bay	Buccaneers Complex	Tampa, Fla.
Washington	Dickinson Coll.	Carlisle, Pa.

The 1963 Minnesota Vikings hold the NFL record for the most fumbles recovered in a season, 58. Of that number, Vikings recovered 27 of their own fumbles while taking possession of 31 opponents' mistakes. Individual honors, if that's the correct term for fumbles lost, go to Oakland quarterback Dan Pastorini. In 1973, while playing with Houston, he committed 17 fumbles—an NFL record.

41. Be it ever so humble . . .

TEAM	STADIUM AND CAPACITY	YEAR OPENED
Atlanta Falcons	Atlanta-Fulton County Stadium (60,748)	1965
Buffalo Bills	Rich Stadium (80,290)	1973
Chicago Bears	Soldier Field (65,790)	1926
Cincinnati Bengals	Riverfront Stadium (59,754)	1970
Cleveland Browns	Cleveland Stadium (80,098)	1932
Dallas Cowboys	Texas Stadium (65,101)	1971
Denver Broncos	Denver Mile High Stadium (75,100)	1948
Detroit Lions	Pontiac Silverdome (80,638)	1975
Green Bay Packers	Lambeau Field (56,155) and Milwaukee County Stadium (55,958)	1957 1953
Houston Oilers	Astrodome (50,000)	1965
Indianapolis Colts	Hossier Dome (61,000)	1983
Kansas City Chiefs	Arrowhead (78,067)	1972
Los Angeles Raiders	Los Angeles Memorial Coliseum (92,510)	1932
Los Angeles Rams	Anaheim Stadium (69,007)	1966
Miami Dolphins	Orange Bowl (75,206)	1938

Minnesota Vikings	Hubert H. Humphrey Metrodome (62,212)	1982
New England Patriots	Sullivan Stadium (61,150)	1971
New Orleans Saints	Louisiana Superdome (71,330)	1975
New York Giants	Giants Stadium (76,891)	1976
New York Jets	Giants Stadium (76,891)	1976
Philadelphia Eagles	Philadelphia Veterans Stadium (73,484)	1971
Pittsburgh Steelers	Three Rivers Stadium (59,000)	1970
St. Louis Cardinals	Busch Memorial Stadium (51,392)	1966
San Diego Chargers	San Diego Jack Murphy Stadium (60,100)	1967
San Francisco 49ers	Candlestick Park (61,185)	1960
Seattle Seahawks	Kingdome (64,757)	1976
Tampa Bay Buccaneers	Tampa Stadium (74,270)	1967
Washington Redskins	Robert F. Kennedy Stadium (55,363)	1961

42. There's more than one way

Fifteen members of the Pro Football Hall of Fame who didn't play in the NFL:

1. Bert Bell .... Commissioner
2. Charles Bidwill, Sr. .... Owner
3. Paul Brown .... Coach
4. Joe Carr .... League President
5. Weeb Ewbank .... Coach
6. Sid Gillman .... Coach
7. Lamar Hunt .... Founder, Owner
8. Vince Lombardi .... Coach
9. George Preston Marshall .... Owner
10. Tim Mara .... Owner
11. Earle (Greasy) Neale .... Coach
12. Hugh (Shorty) Ray .... Supervisor of Officials
13. Dan Reeves .... Owner
14. Art Rooney, Sr. .... Owner
15. Pete Rozelle .... Commissioner

43. Take me out to the ballgame

Six former NFL teams:

TEAM	YEAR
. Cleveland Indians	1921 and 1923
2. New York Yankees	1927–28
3. Brooklyn Dodgers	1930–1943
4. Boston Braves	1932
5. Pittsburgh Pirates	1933–39
6. Texas Rangers*	1952

* When the franchise was awarded, the team was known as the Texas Rangers, but the name was changed to the Dallas Texans before the start of the 1952 season (two other NFL teams with major league baseball counterparts are the New York Giants and the St. Louis Cardinals).

44. Sometimes not even a bridesmaid

Six NFL teams that have never won a league or world championship:

1. Atlanta Falcons
2. Cincinnati Bengals
3. New England Patriots
4. New Orleans Saints
5. Seattle Seahawks
6. Tampa Bay Buccaneers

Three former NFL players have served in the U.S. House of Representatives. Lavern Dilweg, an end with the Milwaukee Badgers (1926) and the Green Bay Packers (1927–1934), ran as a Democrat in Wisconsin and was elected for a single term, 1940–42. Chet Chesney, a center from DePaul with the Chicago Bears (1939–1940), served one term in the House of Representatives as a Democrat from Illinois (1948–1950). Jack Kemp, a former quarterback with the Pitssburgh Steelers (1957). Los Angeles Chargers (1960), San Diego Chargers (1961–62), and Buffalo Bills (1962–69), now serves as a Republican from New York State.

45. Big Apple big time

Professional football franchises in New York City:

TEAM AND LEAGUE	YEAR
New York Giants (NFL)	1925-present
Brooklyn Horsemen (AFL)	1926
Brooklyn Lions (NFL)	1926
New York Yankees (AFL)	1926
New York Yankees (NFL)	1927-28
Stapleton Stapes (NFL)	1929-32
Brooklyn Dodgers (NFL)	1930-43
Brooklyn Tigers (AFL)	1936
New York Yankees (AFL)	1936
New York Yankees (AFL)	1940
New York Americans (AFL)	1941
Brooklyn Tigers (NFL)	1944
Brooklyn Dodgers (AAFC)	1946-48
New York Yankees (AAFC)	1946-48
Brooklyn-N.Y. Yankees (AAFC)	1949
New York Bulldogs (NFL)	1949
New York Yanks (NFL)	1950-51
New York (Titans) Jets (NFL-AFL)	1960-present
New York Stars (WFL)	1974

46. The big ones that got away

Six quarterbacks who were (briefly) Pittsburgh Steelers:

1. Len Dawson
2. Jack Kemp
3. Sid Luckman
4. Earl Morrall
5. Bill Nelson
6. Johnny Unitas

47. O.K., but just for a year or two

Thirteen Houston Oilers head coaches in the team's 25-year history:

COACH	YEARS	RECORD
Lou Rymkus	1960–61	11-7-1
Wally Lemm	1961	9-0-0
Frank (Pop) Ivy	1962–63	17-11-0
Sammy Baugh	1964	4-10-0
Hugh (Bones) Taylor	1965	4-10-0
Wally Lemm	1966–70	28-38-4
Ed Hughes	1971	4-9-1
Bill Peterson	1972–73	1-18-0
Sid Gillman	1973–74	8-15-0
O.A. (Bum) Phillips	1975–80	59-38-0
Ed Biles	1981–83	8-23-0
Chuck Studley	1983	2-8-0
Hugh Campbell	1984	3-13-0

48. Wire to wire

Longest plays:
   Kickoff return: 106 yards, Roy Green, St. Louis vs. Dallas, 1979; Noland Smith, Kansas City vs. Denver, 1967; Al Carmichael, Green Bay vs. Chicago Bears, 1956.
Fumble return: 104 yards, Jack Tatum, Oakland vs. Green Bay, 1972.
Interception return: 102 yards, Gary Barbaro, Kansas City vs. Seattle, 1977; Erich Barnes, New York Giants vs. Dallas, 1961; Bob Smith, Detroit vs. Chicago Bears, 1949.
Pass play: 99 yards, Sonny Jurgensen to Gerry Allen, Washington vs. Chicago, 1968; Karl Sweetan to Pat Studstill, Detroit vs. Baltimore, 1966; George Izo to Bobby Mitchell, Washington vs. Cleveland, 1963; Frankie Filchock to Andy Farkas, Washington vs. Pittsburgh, 1939.
Punt return: 98 yards, Dennis Morgan, Dallas vs. St. Louis, 1974; Charlie West, Minnesota vs. Washington, 1968; Gil LeFebvre, Cincinnati vs. Brooklyn, 1933.
Run from scrimmage: 99 yards, Tony Dorsett, Dallas vs. Minnesota, 1982.

49. Jock in the booth

Fifteen former NFL players who are now sportscasters:

1. Terry Bradshaw
2. Tom Brookshier
3. John Brodie
4. Irv Cross
5. Len Dawson
6. Frank Gifford
7. Paul Hornung
8. Don Meredith
9. Johnny Morris
10. Merlin Olsen
11. O.J. Simpson
12. Roger Staubach
13. Pat Summerall
14. Fran Tarkenton
15. Tim Van Galder

50. Officially speaking

From 1938–1946 the NFL presented its only "official" Most Valuable Player Trophy. It was named in honor of Joe F. Carr, the league's president from 1921–1939. Winners were:

1938   Mel Hein, center, New York Giants
1939   Parker Hall, halfback, Cleveland Rams
1940   Ace Parker, halfback, Brooklyn Dodgers
1941   Don Hutson, end, Green Bay Packers
1942   Don Hutson, end, Green Bay Packers
1943   Sid Luckman, quarterback, Chicago Bears
1944   Frank Sinkwich, halfback, Detroit Lions
1945   Bob Waterfield, quarterback, Cleveland Rams
1946   Bill Dudley, halfback, Pittsburgh Steelers

Answers

Answers to "NFL Trivia Quiz"

1. d
2. b
3. e
4. b
5. b
6. b
7. c. Bezdek managed the Pittsburgh Pirates in 1917, 1918, and 1919 and coached the Cleveland Rams in 1937 and 1938.
8. a. Merlin Olsen, b. Alan Page, c. Joe Greene, d. Manny Fernandez, e. Ed (Too Tall) Jones.
9. False. Willie Wood is not an enshrinee, but Willie Brown is.
10. Joe (The Jet) Perry played for Compton J.C. Dick (Night Train) Lane played for Scottsbluff J.C.
11. f
12. c
13. a. Curley Culp was an NCAA heavyweight wrestling champion at Arizona State.
14. d. Hank Soar played for the New York Giants (1937–44 and 1946), umpired in the American League (1950–71), and coached the Providence Steamrollers in the BAA, a forerunner to the NBA (1947–48).
15. c
16. b
17. d
18. b. Smith, a quarterback from Alabama, played with the Redskins from 1936–38. Jay Berwanger, the first overall choice in the draft, elected not to play.
19. a
20. a
21. e
22. b

23. c
24. b
25. 1-i, 2-b, 3-a, 4-h, 5-j, 6-f, 7-d, 8-e, 9-g, 10-c.
26. a
27. b
28. They all played quarterback in the NFL after playing college football for Don Coryell at San Diego State.
29. b
30. c
31. d
32. e
33. c
34. c
35. c
36. Los Angeles Rams, Detroit Lions, Chicago Bears, Indianpolis Colts, Cincinnati Bengals, Denver Broncos, and Miami Dolphins.
37. b
38. False. The only teams to do it were the Philadelphia Eagles of 1948 and 1949. They shut out the Chicago Cardinals 7–0 in 1948 and the Los Angeles Rams 14–0 in 1949.
39. d
40. c
41. a. Ewbank coached the 1958 and 1959 Baltimore Colts and the 1968 New York Jets to world titles.
42. b
43. d
44. False. George McAfee, Chicago Bears Hall of Fame halfback 1940–1950) is the all-time leader with an average of 12.78 yards per punt return.
45. False. Gillom's 43.8 yard average ranks fourth on the all-time list behind Sammy Baugh's 45.1, Tommy Davis's 44.7, and Yale Lary's 44.3
46. b. Albert played with the 49ers from 1946–1952.

47. True
48. a
49. False. Foreman led the NFC in scoring and receiving but finished second by six yards to Jim Otis of the Cardinals in rushing.
50. Offense: 1-g, 2-j, 3-e, 4-h, 5-a, 6-d, 7-b, 8-k, 9-f, 10-i, 11-c.
    Defense: 1-e, 2-j, 3-a, 4-g, 5-i, 6-h, 7-k, 8-c, 9-f, 10-b, 11-d
51. Elmer Layden. Predecessors Jim Thorpe, Joe Carr, and Carl Storck all held the title of President. The other three Horsemen were quarterback Harry Stuldreher, half-back Jim Crowley, and fullback Don Miller.
52. b
53. True
54. Big Ten: 1-j, 2-h, 3-b, 4-a, 5-d, 6-c, 7-f, 8-e, 9-g, 10-i;
    Pac-10: 1-j, 2-i, 3-h, 4-g, 5-e, 6-f, 7-c, 8-d, 9-b, 10-a;
    Big Eight: 1-b, 2-c, 3-d, 4-f, 5-a, 6-g, 7-e, 8-h;
    Southwestern Conference: 1-c, 2-d, 3-e, 4-g, 5-f, 6-i, 7-h, 8-b, 9-a;
    Southeastern Conference; 1-b, 2-d, 3-f, 4-i, 5-a, 6-h, 7-e, 8-j, 9-c, 10-g;
    Independents: 1-d, 2-j, 3-a, 4-h, 5-c, 6-e, 7-g, 8-i, 9-f, 10.b
55. b
56. Brooklyn Dodgers, Buffalo Bisons, Chicago Rockets, Cleveland Browns, Los Angeles Dons, Miami Seahawks, New York Yankees, and San Francisco 49ers.
57. b
58. False. Gale Sayers, with a 30.6 average, is the all-time leader.
59. a
60. True
61. a
62. e

63. b. The move was made in 1937.
64. f. Both Gent (a wide receiver from Michigan State) and Green (a cornerback from Utah State) had played basketball in college.
65. False. There are seven: referee, umpire, head lines-man, line judge, field judge, back judge, and side judge.
66. e
67. c
68. c.
69. f
70. False. Minnesota's Paul Krause moved ahead of Tunnell in 1979. Krause's total is 81, Tunnell's 79.
71. e
72. e
73. d
74. d
75. d. Gary McDermott, a second-year running back, was already wearing number 32, but he gave up the number in time for Simpson to wear it in the first regular season game of 1969.
76. e
77. e. Kenny passed for 4,348 yards.
78. c
79. b
80. f. The Redskins won the game.
81. True
82. b
83. False. The Youngbloods are not even related.
84. d
85. True. The other AFL's existed in 1926, 1936–37, and 1940–41.
86. a
87. 1-g, 2-d, 3-c, 4-h, 5-j, 6-a, 7-e, 8-i, 9-f, 10-b,
88. St. Louis Cardinals, Philadelphia Eagles, Seattle Seahawks, and Atlanta Falcons.

89. c

90. f. Simpson gained 2,003 yards in 1973.

91. c. Blanda, playing for Houston, threw for 36 touchdowns in 1961. He was intercepted 42 times in 1962.

92. b. The Packers have won 11 league titles: 1929, 1930, 1931, 1936, 1939, 1944, 1961, 1962, 1965, 1966, and 1967.

93. e. Dickerson gained 1,803 yards.

94. c. The Browns set the record during their 42–21 victory over the Chicago Bears in 1951.

95. d. Dempsey's kick was 63 yards.

96. f. The Tampa Bay Buccaneers lost the first 26 games they ever played; all 14 in 1976 and the first 12 of 1977.

97. c. In 1975 Metcalf gained 2,462 yards in the following categories: rushing, 816 yards; receiving, 378; punt returns, 285; kickoff returns, 960. He also advanced a fumble 23 yards.

98. d. Thrower played for the Chicago Bears in 1953.

99. b. Contrary to trivia legend, Y.A. Tittle was not a third member of the LSU backfield at that time.

100. f. As youngsters, the brother and sister were playing and Jeanne told Erny of a vision she had of his becoming a famous football player. He was an All-America at USC and played with the Boston/Washington Redskins, 1932–40.

101. f. Carson admits to being hooked on such soaps as "The Edge of Night," "As the World Turns," and "The Secret Storm" since childhood.

102. Fouts attempted 609 passes, completing 360 for 4,802 yards.

103. c. Brown led the NFL in eight of the nine seasons he played.

104. f. Moore scored in the final two games of the 1963 season, all 14 games of 1964, and the first two of 1965.

105. c. As an expansion team the Cowboys could not partici-
pate in the NFL draft. They signed Perkins (a halfback
from New Mexico) and Meredith (a quarterback from
Southern Methodist) to personal services contracts and
acquired their rights (Perkins from the Baltimore Colts
and Meredith from the Chicago Bears).
106. f. Grupp averaged 43.6 yards on 89 punts. His net
average of 37.2 led the league in that category.
107. e. Harder, who played with the Chicago Cardinals
(1946–1950), and the Detroit Lions (1951–53) made
nine PATs against the New York Giants in 1948. He
was an NFL official for 17 seasons.
108. b
109. c. Hultz, a defensive tackle, made nine recoveries with
the Minnesota Vikings in 1963.
110. d. The 49ers attempted 602 passes and completed 361
for 3,760 yards. In 1981 Minnesota passed 709 times,
completing 382 for 4,567 yards.
111. a. Sam Cunningham gained 768 yards, Horace Ivory
693, Andy Johnson 675, and Steve Grogan 539.
112. False. Although the Super Bowl was televised by two
networks, the networks were NBC, which did the AFL
regular season games, and CBS, which showed the
NFL regular season.
113. e. Fred Williamson referred to his karate-like forearm
chop as "the hammer" and speculated that he might
just wipe out the entire Packers' offense.
114. c
115. b
116. False. The Pittsburgh Steelers won their first Super
Bowl appearance, game IX, the San Francisco 49ers won
in game XVI.
117. c
118. False. Joe Kapp was the quarterback when the Vikings
lost Super Bowl IV to the Kansas City Chiefs.

119. c
120. a. The controversy arose over whether or not Renfro touched the ball. If he didn't—and he maintained he did not—it would have been illegal under then-existing rules for two members of the offensive team (Hinton and Mackey) to touch the ball without a member of the defense touching it.
121. b
122. d. Alworth spent most of his career with the Chargers; Ditka with the Bears and Eagles.
123. d
124. b
125. False. Larry Cole, Cliff Harris, D.D. Lewis, Preston Pearson, Charlie Waters, and Rayfield Wright also have played in five Super Bowls.
126. d. The 17 net yards yielded by the Steelers defense still stands as a Super Bowl record.
127. a
128. b
129. False. Although Pearson played in five Super Bowls, he did it with only three teams—Colts, Steelers, and Cowboys.
130. True
131. c. Brown's return is a Super Bowl record.
132. True
133. b
134. c
135. True. The Cowboys had won VI and XII, the Steelers IX and X.
136. True. Cole started at left defensive end in Super Bowl V, right defensive tackle in game X, and left defensive tackle in game XIII.
137. True
138. True.

139. d. Dallas linebacker Chuck Howley (the only player from a losing team so honored) won the award in Super Bowl V.

140. d. Harris won the award in Super Bowl IX, Csonka in VIII, Riggins in XVII, and Allen XVIII.

141. False. Safety Jake Scott, Miami Dolphins, was presented with the award for Super Bowl VII.

142. False. Swann won in Super Bowl X, Fred Biletnikoff of the Raiders won in Super Bowl XI, and Stallworth has not won the award.

143. d. It was the Minnesota Vikings' rallying cry for Super Bowl IV.

144. b

145. True. Dwight White in Super Bowl IX, and Reggie Harrison in Super Bowl X.

146. False. Tom Landry's two Super Bowl victories were in VI and XII.

147. False. Don Shula took the Colts and the Dolphins to the Super Bowl.

148. False. The leading interceptors are linebackers Chuck Howley of the Dallas Cowboys and Rod Martin of the Raiders.

149. False. Landry has lost three of the five games the Cowboys have played, but Bud Grant has lost all four of the Minnesota Vikings' Super Bowl games.

150. False. Super Bowl VIII was played in Rice Stadium, Houston, Texas.

Answers to "You Make the Call"

1. d. The fumble was in the end zone. When a foul occurs during a fumble, as it did on this play, enforcement of the foul is from the spot of the fumble. If the offense (in this case, San Diego) commits a

foul *anywhere,* and the spot of enforcement is behind its goal line, it is ruled a safety.

2. b. If a member of the offensive team lifts a runner to his feet, it is ruled illegal use of hands. The penalty is 15 yards from the spot of the foul.

3. c. It is a foul if a player pushes an opponent, unless it is in a legal *personal* attempt to recover a loose ball. On this play, a Detroit player pushed an opponent, not in a personal attempt to recover the ball but to enable a teammate to recover it. This is ruled a defensive foul for illegal use of hands. The penalty is five yards. It is enforced from the spot of the previous snap (4-yard line). Any defensive foul behind the spot of the previous snap is enforced from that spot (i.e., in this case, the 4).

4. b. The kicker kicked a loose ball, which is a foul. The ball went over the end line after it crossed the crossbar. This is ruled a touchback, as the kicking team has put the ball out of its opponents' end zone. Had the kicker been able to gain full possession of the ball, he would have been permitted to drop-kick it, for example.

5. b. It was a safety. The ball is ruled dead when it hits the shaft of the goal marker, which is considered out-of-bounds. Therefore, Dallas fell on a dead ball in the end zone, which had no bearing on the play. Washington had possession of the ball last, before it went out-of-bounds. On a fumble out-of-bounds, possession goes to the team that last controlled the ball. In this case, the ball was declared out-of-bounds, and Washington had put the ball into its own end zone, thereby creating a safety. The offensive clip (by Washington), as the ball was rolling loose, further confused the issue. The kickoff following the safety should be from the Redskins' 10-yard line rather than from its 20, as is customary following a safety. On a scoring play, when a personal foul occurs and

the foul didn't contribute to the score, the penalty is assessed on the next kickoff. A clip is a personal foul.

6. c. This was an illegal forward pass, as it was thrown from beyond the line of scrimmage. The penalty for the foul is loss of down and five yards from the spot of the illegal pass.

7. c. This is considered a free kick (kickoff) out of bounds. When the Atlanta player recovered the ball with one foot on the sideline, the play was dead. The last player to have touched the ball before it went out of bounds was a Falcon. If a member of the kicking team (offensive team) is the last player to have touched the ball before it goes out of bounds, it is ruled a re-kick with a five-yard penalty. If the defensive team is the last one to touch the kickoff ball before it goes out of bounds, the ball is awarded to the defensive team at the spot where it goes out.

8. c. This is considered an illegal forward pass thrown from beyond the line of scrimmage. This type of pass calls for a five-yard penalty from the spot of the pass and a loss of down. However, Minnesota made more than enough for the first down, and after the ball was placed on the 10-yard line, the Vikings still had their first down. When the forward pass (though illegal) hit the ground, the ball was dead, and no further action could take place on that ball. Therefore, Detroit recovered a dead ball, so the Lions couldn't take possession legally.

9. d. The Minnesota player who threw the ball down in his own end zone was actually throwing a backward pass. If a backward pass hits the ground, the ball is not dead. In this case, the ball rolled out to the 2-yard line, where the Bears recovered. That's legal, but a backward pass that hits the ground can not be advanced by the defensive team if they recover it. In this situation, the ball is dead where it is recovered. A backward pass is defined as any pass that is not a forward pass. A forward pass is one that moves

toward the opponent's goal line. The pass on this play was toward the Minnesota player's own goal line and therefore was a backward pass.

10. c. This is considered a foul during a running play. The foul occurred on the 2-yard line. The NFC is awarded possession and a first down on the AFC's 1-yard line (half the distance to the goal). The spot of enforcement for a foul on a running play, if the foul occurs at the end of the run, is the spot of the foul. If the NFC player merely had fumbled and there had been no foul, it would have been a touchback.

11. d. The move was an illegal forward pass, as the ball was handed forward on a play that was not begun at scrimmage. The penalty is five yards from the spot of the pass (forward handoff, in this case). The ball is dead when handed forward and possessed by the second ball handler. If the second Ram had *dropped* the ball after the handoff, it also would have been ruled a dead ball.

12. a. A player may use his hands in a personal legal attempt to recover a loose ball. If the Ram had pushed the Bill out of the way to enable one of his teammates to recover the ball, it would have been illegal use of hands. The ball then would return to Buffalo with a first down. However, this play is legal all the way.

13. b. It is a touchdown, not pass interference. Pass interference rules do not apply to an illegal pass unless it is a second pass from behind the line of scrimmage. This was an illegal pass, as the passer threw the ball from beyond scrimmage. Illegal passes may be intercepted.

14. b. The ball must touch the ground beyond the receiving team's restraining line, which in this case was Chicago's 45-yard line, or be touched by a member of the receiving team, in order for either side to take possession.

15. d. No player of the kicking team may touch a scrimmage kick before it has been touched by a receiver. If an illegal touch occurs, it is ruled the receivers' ball at the spot of illegal touching, which in this case was Green Bay's 32. Though the punt was partially blocked, it remained a kicked ball because it crossed the line of scrimmage and was not touched by a Chicago player beyond that point. A Green Bay player was the first to touch the kicked ball beyond the line of scrimmage, thus it became Chicago's ball at the spot of the illegal touch, the 32.

16. d. This was a fourth down fumble play. Cleveland's holder was the player considered to have fumbled the ball. The fourth down fumble rule states that if a fourth down fumble occurs and the recovery is by another offensive player, the spot of the next snap is the spot of the fumble, unless the spot of recovery is behind the spot of the fumble, in which case it becomes the spot of recovery. Cleveland's holder was not eligible to recover the ball, as no defensive player touched it after the holder fumbled on Cincinnati's 9. The Browns' kicker picked up the ball behind the spot of the fumble, so the ball is dead there. Cleveland didn't make the necessary yardage for a first down, so Cincinnati takes over on its 12-yard line.

17. c. This was a foul on a running play with a change of possession (from Cardinals to Redskins). If a foul occurs during a running play (which this was, because the Cardinals' ball carrier ran from scrimmage), and the run on which the foul occurs is followed by a change of possession, the spot of enforcement is the spot of the foul. The foul (defensive holding) took place at the Redskins' 40-yard line, and the penalty for that foul is five yards.

18. c. If a legal receiver goes out of bounds accidentally or is forced out by a defender, and he (the receiver) returns to touch or catch a pass inbounds, the play is treated as a pass touched or caught out of bounds.

No penalty yardage is involved. No pass interference is called on an action involving an ineligible receiver, which was what the Cleveland running back became when he went out of bounds, so the Houston linebacker's shove was nothing. The pass should be ruled incomplete.

19. b. The defensive team would logically refuse both the illegal bat and the offside, making the situation fourth down. New Orleans would then have to punt, giving up the ball. If the defensive team were to accept either penalty, the situation would be third down again. That would give New Orleans an opportunity to try for a first down.

20. a. The Chargers' quarterback threw a second forward pass from behind the line of scrimmage. The ruling is loss of down, and the ball is placed at the spot of the previous snap. A second forward pass is an illegal pass. In this case, when it was caught, the play was over. The subsequent fumble recovery didn't count.

21. c. A missed field goal from outside the 20-yard line returns to the spot where it was snapped. If the ball had touched a 49er in the field of play, and then the Rams' tight end had fallen on it, it would have been the Rams' ball there.

22. d. This was intentional grounding of a forward pass. The penalty is 15 yards and a loss of down. Because the play started from the 4-yard line, the penalty goes to the 2 (half the distance to the goal, in this case) with a loss of down.

23. b. Because the fullback never had possession of the backward pass, it remained a backward pass. No defensive player may advance a backward pass if he recovers the ball after it touches the ground. The ball is dead where it is recovered. Because the fullback was the person responsible for putting the ball into Miami's end zone and it was recovered there by Miami, it is a touchback. The ball is put in play by Miami with a first down at its 20.

24. b. The return man put the ball into his own end zone after having caught it in the field of play.

25. c. This is considered a backward pass, not a fumble. A backward pass may be advanced by the defense only if the ball is caught in flight. No defensive player may advance a backward pass if he recovers the ball after it touches the ground. In that case, the ball is dead where it is recovered. The recovering team takes over at the spot of recovery. It is legal for a player to push an opponent out of the way and to use his hands in an actual attempt to recover a loose ball.

26. b. Though kicking a loose ball is a violation, it is penalized from the kickoff spot, because it still is a kick. Denver would naturally refuse the penalty to keep the ball. The Broncos can only recover the ball, not advance it, because Houston never had possessed it. The penalty against Denver for holding would be ignored because it took place during a dead ball and therefore wasn't a personal foul. The ball became dead when it was recovered by the kicking team.

27. c. When a team commits a personal foul (e.g., roughing the passer) prior to the completion of a legal forward pass from behind the line of scrimmage, the offended team benefits from a 15-yard penalty enforced from the spot where the ball is dead beyond the line of scrimmage. The exception to the rule is that if the offended team (Denver) loses possession after a completion, enforcement is from where possession was lost (in this case, the Cowboys' 40-yard line), and the ball reverts to the offended team.

28. d. This was defensive holding against the Colts on a running play. When the spot of enforcement is behind the line of scrimmage, as was the case here, any penalty yardage is assessed from the spot of the previous snap. A defensive holding penalty is five yards. This was not pass interference because the ball never was thrown.

29. d. St. Louis threw an illegal pass. The passer went

beyond the line of scrimmage and threw from the 7. There is no defensive pass interference on an illegal pass. The ball became dead when it hit the goal post, so the St. Louis receiver caught a dead ball. The penalty against St. Louis for a pass thrown from behind the line of scrimmage is loss of down and five yards from the spot of the pass. The ball was thrown from the 7-yard line on fourth down. It then became Pittsburgh's ball, first down on the Steelers' 12.

30. b. Both of the defensive back's feet would have had to touch in the field of play for "intercepting momentum" to have been ruled. The player's second step took him and the ball into the end zone. Had his second foot touched in the field of play, and had he carried the ball (due to "intercepting momentum") into the end zone, the ball would have gone back to where he intercepted it (the Rams' 2).

THE SECOND OFFICIAL

NFL TRIVIA
BOOK

Jim Campbell

All contents are accurate as of February 15, 1985

Contents

NFL Trivia Quiz II

More trivia of NFL history in over 150 questions, lists, and random items

1. Escort Service

Match the NFL player in the first column with his blocking back in college in the second column:

1. Ricky Bell, USC   a. Lynn Cain
2. Joe Cribbs, Auburn   b. Mosi Tatupi
3. Archie Griffin, Ohio State   c. William Andrews
4. Charles White, USC   d. Pete Johnson

2. Long-Playing Record

Which player set an NFL record by scoring 40 points in one game?

   a. Frankie Albert, 49ers, 1951
   b. Jim Brown, Browns, 1962
   c. Paul Hornung, Packers, 1960
   d. Dub Jones, Browns, 1953
   e. Ernie Nevers, Chicago Cardinals, 1929
   f. Gale Sayers, Bears, 1965

3. Don't Call Me Johnson

Fill in the first name.

1. _____, Johnson, CB, Steelers
2. _____, Johnson, K, Seahawks
3. _____, Johnson, DE, Packers
4. _____, Johnson, S, Rams
5. _____, Johnson, RB, Chargers
6. _____, Johnson, NT, Vikings
7. _____, Johnson, DT, Chargers
8. _____, Johnson, WR, Oilers
9. _____, Johnson, LB, Buccaneers
10. _____, Johnson, DE, Bills
11. _____, Johnson, CB, Falcons
12. _____, Johnson, TE, Dolphins

4. Man of Letters

Which nationally syndicated newspaper columnist and Chicago television personality once played in the NFL?

   a. Burt Bacharach
   b. Bob Considine
   c. Irv Kupcinet
   d. John O'Hara
   e. Grantland Rice
   f. Walter Winchell

Revolving Door

The first year the New England Patriots (known as the Boston Patriots in 1960) held their training camp at the University of Massachusetts in Amherst, 350 different candidates were given tryouts. The player limit in 1960 was 35.

5. I Get Around

Which of the NFL players below is the only one *not* to make the Pro Bowl with three different teams?

   a. Sam Baker, kicker, Redskins, Cowboys, and Eagles
   b. Erich Barnes, cornerback, Bears, Giants, and Browns
   c. Bob Brown, tackle, Eagles, Rams, and Raiders
   d. Ted Hendricks, linebacker, Colts, Packers, and Raiders
   e. Jim Ringo, center, Steelers, Packers, and Eagles
   f. Norman Snead, quarterback, Redskins, Eagles, and Giants

6. Switch Hitter

Which former NFL head coach, who also played pro football, was the president of baseball's New York Yankees?

   a. George Allen
   b. Howard (Hopalong) Cassady
   c. Ralph Houk
   d. George Steinbrenner
   e. Gene Michaels
   f. Lou Saban

7. The Ultimate Post Pattern

Which passing combination set a record for the longest touchdown pass in the NFL since the league was realigned in 1970?

- a. Terry Bradshaw to Lynn Swann, Steelers
- b. Pat Haden to Wendell Tyler, Rams
- c. Jim Plunkett to Cliff Branch, Raiders
- d. Gifford Nielsen to Mike Renfro, Oilers
- e. Phil Simms to Earnest Gray, Giants
- f. Richard Todd to Johnny (Lam) Jones, Jets

8. Bench Warmer

The New York judge who presided over the Clifford Irving trial (the Howard Hughes "fake" biography lawsuit) was once a guard with the New York Giants. Name him.

- a. John Cannella
- b. Denver (Butch) Gibson
- c. Sam Huff
- d. Jack Stroud
- e. Byron (Whizzer) White
- f. Len Younce

Learning Their ABCs at Auburn

During the 1978 college football season, Auburn's backfield included present-day NFL running backs William Andrews of the Falcons, James Brooks of the Chargers, and Joe Cribbs of the Bills.

9. Legacy

Which NFL player's grandfather served as president of the university the player attended?

   a. Curtis Brown, Bills
   b. Gary Dunn, Steelers
   c. Cornell Green, Cowboys
   d. Yale Lary, Lions
   e. Danny Villaneuva, Cowboys
   f. Joe Washington, Redskins

10. Every Litter Bit Hurts

Tom Skladany of the Lions, who led the NFL in punting in 1981 with a 43.5 yard average and a 37.3 net average, earned which of the following nicknames while in college?

   a. Beer Can
   b. Bud Man
   c. Rainmaker
   d. Roof Breaker
   e. Sky King
   f. Trashman

11. College of Cardinals

In 1971, how many ex-Stanford quarterbacks were starting in the NFL?

    a. None
    b. 1
    c. 2
    d. 3
    e. 4
    f. 5

12. Star Warriors

What is the correct term for the three starlike figures that appear on the Pittsburgh Steelers' helmet logo?

    a. Hexagons
    b. Hypocycloids
    c. Octagons
    d. Parabolas
    e. Pentagons
    f. Trapezoids

Every Tom, Dick, and Craig

Since 1960, the following 33 players have at one time been quarterbacks for the Denver Broncos.

Don Breaux, 1963	Jim LeClair, 1967–68
Marlin Briscoe, 1968	Jacky Lee, 1964–65
Scott Brunner, 1984	Pete Liske, 1969–1970
Max Choboian, 1966	John McCormick, 1963,
Steve DeBerg, 1981	1965–66, 1968
Joe DiVito, 1968	Craig Morton, 1977–1981
John Elway, 1983	Alan Pastrana, 1969–1970
Hunter Enis, 1962	Craig Penrose, 1976–79
Mike Ernst, 1972	Steve Ramsey, 1971–76
Scotty Glacken, 1966–67	Matt Robinson, 1980
Mark Herrmann, 1981–82	Tobin Rote, 1966
George Herring, 1960–61	George Shaw, 1962
Don Horn, 1971–72	Mickey Slaughter, 1963–66
John Hufnagel, 1974–75	Steve Tensi, 1967–1970
Charley Johnson, 1972–75	Frank Tripucka, 1960–63
Jeff Knapple, 1980	Norris Weese, 1976–79
Gary Kubiak, 1983–84	Dick Wood, 1962

Permanent Residents

Since 1947, the Cleveland Browns have had only three starting left offensive tackles.

Lou Groza*	1947–1959
Dick Schafrath	1960–1971
Doug Dieken	1972 to date

*In 1946, the Browns' first year, Groza shared some playing time with Chet Adams, Ernie Blandin, and Lou Rymkus.

13. Stingy

Which team allowed its opponents an all-time low 20 points in 13 games during the 1927 season?

- a. Dayton Triangles
- b. Duluth Eskimos
- c. Frankford Yellowjackets
- d. Green Bay Packers
- e. New York Giants
- f. Providence Steamroller

14. First, If Not Foremost

Name the first black quarterback of the Tampa Bay Buccaneers.

- a. Parnell Dickinson
- b. Karl Douglas
- c. James Harris
- d. Matt Reed
- e. Willie Thrower
- f. Doug Williams

15. Even Sam Could Miss This One

In the 1961 television special "The Violent World of Sam Huff," the Giants Pro Football Hall of Fame middle linebacker was heard admonishing a young Chicago Bears tight end, "You better watch that, number eighty-eight. Watch that stuff, eighty-eight. Knock it off, eighty-eight." Which player was the Bears' 88?

    a. Willard Dewveall
    b. Mike Ditka
    c. Ron Kramer
    d. Ed O'Bradovich
    e. Reggie Rucker
    f. Lionel Taylor

16. Son Devils

Which men, whose fathers were pro athletes, formed the shortstop-second base combination for the Arizona State baseball team in the early 1970s?

    a. George Brett and John Jefferson
    b. Glenn Carano and Steve Garvey
    c. Phil Garner and Mark Malone
    d. Tony Hill and Dave Winfield
    e. Thurman Munson and Dave Logan
    f. Bump Wills and Danny White

17. Tails You Lose

Which Pro Football Hall of Fame tackle ended his career when he twisted his knee as he turned to go back to the sidelines after a pregame coin toss?

a. Johnny Blood (McNally), Packers
b. Glen (Turk) Edwards, Redskins
c. Forrest Gregg, Packers
d. Lou Groza, Browns
e. Walt Kiesling, Packers
f. Jim Parker, Colts

Homebody

Until the 1980 season, when the Los Angeles Rams moved to Anaheim Stadium, running back Wendell Tyler played all of his home football games within a three-mile radius—first at Los Angeles's Crenshaw High School, then at UCLA, and then with the Rams in 1978–79. Both UCLA and the Rams played in the Los Angeles Coliseum. Trivia on trivia: Crenshaw, UCLA, and the Rams all have blue and gold as team colors.

18. Yeah, But Does He Have a Curve Ball?

Bob Waterfield, the Rams' Pro Football Hall of Fame quarterback of the 1940s and 1950s, once had the speed of a pass clocked for a distance of 60 feet. How fast did the ball travel over the approximate distance from a baseball pitching mound to home plate?

   a. about 20 miles per hour
   b. more than 50 miles per hour
   c. more than 60 miles per hour
   d. more than 80 miles per hour
   e. 98.6 miles per hour
   f. more than 100 miles per hour

19. 1,000 Giant Steps Forward

Which running back is the only New York Giant ever to gain more than 1,000 yards in a season?

   a. Rob Carpenter
   b. Tucker Frederickson
   c. Frank Gifford
   d. Hinkey Haines
   e. Ron Johnson
   f. Eddie Price

20. T-Boner

Which NFL team was the last to switch to the modern T-formation?

    a. Brooklyn Dodgers, 1941
    b. Chicago Bears, 1940
    c. Detroit Lions, 1944
    d. Pittsburgh Steelers, 1952
    e. Portsmouth Spartans, 1932
    f. Washington Redskins, 1937

21. Draft Dodgers

Which two members of the Pro Football Hall of Fame first came into the NFL as free agents, rather than as draft choices?

    a. Herb Adderley and Lance Alworth
    b. Bill Dudley and Clarence (Ace) Parker
    c. Dick (Night Train) Lane and Emlen Tunnell
    d. Gino Marchetti and Ray Nitschke
    e. Merlin Olsen and Jim Parker
    f. Gale Sayers and Larry Wilson

Could This Be the Bard Himself?

In 1936 the Steelers drafted William Shakespeare, a quarterback from Notre Dame, on the first round. Known as just plain Bill, Shakespeare did not play in the NFL.

22. New Faces of 1984

The Cincinnati Bengals, Green Bay Packers, Houston Oilers, and Minnesota Vikings named new head coaches for 1984. Which men filled the positions?

a. George Allen, Hugh Campbell, Walt Michaels, and Chuck Knox

b. Hugh Campbell, Les Steckel, Sam Wyche, and Ed Biles

c. Sam Wyche, Chuck Hutchinson, Jim Mora, and Forrest Gregg

d. George Perles, Carl Peterson, Bobby Knight, and Les Steckel

e. Joe Walton, Joe Gibbs, Chuck Noll, and Chuck Knox

f. Hugh Campbell, Forrest Gregg, Les Steckel, and Sam Wyche

23. Veteran of Domestic Wars

Who was the first player drafted by the American Football League prior to its inaugural (1960) season?

a. Richie Lucas, quarterback, Penn State—Buffalo Bills

b. Billy Cannon, running back, Louisiana State—Houston Oilers

c. Mike Hudock, center, Miami—New York Titans

d. Johnny Robinson, running back, Louisiana State—Dallas Texans

e. George Blanda, quarterback, Kentucky—Houston Oilers

f. Larry Wilson, safety, Utah—Oakland Raiders

24. Two-fers

At the start of the 1982 NFL season, two NFC teams were able to "save" a spot on their roster because one of their kickers was also used in another capacity. Which players fill two positions?

a. Frank Corral, Rams, and Danny White, Cowboys
b. Steve Cox, Browns, and Mel Gray, Cardinals
c. Rick Danmeier, Vikings, and Phil Simms, Giants
d. Mark Moseley, Redskins, and Jack Rudnay, Chiefs
e. John Smith, Patriots, and Keith Fahnhorst, 49ers
f. Jan Stenerud, Packers, and John Bunting, Eagles

25. Hooray for Houston

Which NFL offensive lineman had a role in the feature film *The Right Stuff?*

a. Anthony Munoz
b. Bubba Smith
c. John Glenn
d. Dick Butkus
e. Mike Webster
f. Jerry Sizemore

They All Grew Up to Be . . .

There are seven men who played for the Cowboys who did not play football in college.

Name	Position	Sport	College
Pete Gent	wide receiver	Basketball	Michigan State
Cornell Green	cornerback	Basketball	Utah State
Percy Howard	wide receiver	Basketball	Austin Peay
Ron Howard	tight end	Basketball	Seattle
Wade Manning	cornerback	Baseball	Ohio State
Preston Pearson	running back	Basketball	Illinois
Colin Ridgway	punter	Track	Lamar Tech

Note: Former Cowboys kicker Toni Fritsch and defensive end John Gonzaga did not attend college.

26. Air Coryell's Pilot

True or False? Quarterback Dan Fouts, who passed for 4,802 yards in 1981, has surpassed 4,000 yards passing three consecutive times. He is the only NFL quarterback ever to pass for more than 4,000 yards

27. When in Doubt . . .

Bob Parsons of the Bears established a new NFL record in 1981 by punting how many times?

   a. 57
   b. 98
   c. 101
   d. 109
   e. 114
   f. 136

28. Trojan Horses

Which of the following offensive linemen did not play at USC?

   a. Bill Bain, guard, Rams
   b. Brad Budde, guard, Chiefs
   c. Don Mosebar, tackle, Raiders
   d. Anthony Munoz, tackle, Bengals
   e. Keith Van Horne, tackle, Bears
   f. Ed White, guard, Chargers

29. The Guys of Texas Are Upon You

Match the NFL offensive players below with the Texas colleges they attended.

1. Johnny (Lam) Jones, WR, Jets	a. Texas Christian
2. David Hill, TE, Rams	b. Texas A&M
3. Cody Risien, T, Browns	c. Texas A&I
4. Kevin Belcher, G, Giants	d. Texas
5. Mike Baab, C, Browns	e. West Texas State
6. John Ayers, G, 49ers	f. Rice
7. Dave Studdard, T, Broncos	g. Texas-El Paso
8. Mike Renfro, WR, Cowboys	h. Texas
9. Tommy Kramer, QB, Vikings	i. Texas
10. Earl Campbell, RB, Oilers	j. Stephen F. Austin
11. Eric Dickerson, RB, Rams	k. Texas
12. Mark Moseley, K. Redskins	l. SMU

Proficient on Either End

In 1943, NFL players went both ways, offense and defense. The top three interception leaders were Sammy Baugh (Redskins) 11, Irv Comp (Packers) 10, and Don Hutson (Packers) 8. Baugh and Comp were passers on offense, with Comp often throwing to end Hutson.

30. Scramblin' Man

Name the NFL quarterback who rushed for nearly 1,000 yards in one season.

    a. Ken Anderson, Bengals, 1981
    b. Bobby Douglas, Bears, 1972
    c. Tobin Rote, Packers, 1951
    d. Fran Tarkenton, Vikings, 1961
    e. Fran Tarkenton, Giants, 1970
    f. Norm Van Brocklin, Eagles, 1959

31. Auspicious Debut

Which rookie running back led the NFL in rushing in 1983 with 1808 yards?

    a. Butch Woolfolk, Giants
    b. Darrin Nelson, Vikings
    c. Curt Warner, Seahawks
    d. Hokie Gajan, Saints
    e. Eric Dickerson, Rams
    f. Sammy Winder, Broncos

32. Johnny Who?

In 1955, Jim Finks and Ted Marchibroda were the Steelers' established quarterbacks. Rookie Johnny Unitas of Louisville was waived by the team. Which player was kept in his place?

   a. Rudy Bukich, USC
   b. Vic Eaton, Missouri
   c. Earl Morrall, Michigan State
   d. Chuck Ortman, Michigan
   e. Jack Scarbath, Maryland
   f. Tommy Wade, Texas

33. Second Season (Second Career)

Which player set an NFL record in 1981 by appearing in his twenty-sixth and twenty-seventh postseason games?

   a. Joe Greene, defensive tackle, Steelers
   b. D.D. Lewis, linebacker, Cowboys
   c. Drew Pearson, wide receiver, Cowboys
   d. Jack Reynolds, linebacker, 49ers
   e. Bill Simpson, safety, Bills
   f. Charlie Waters, safety, Cowboys

Myth-conception

The first player taken in the 1965 American Football League draft was not Joe Namath, quarterback, Alabama. It was Lawrence Elkins, wide receiver, Baylor. Elkins, whose career was shortened by injuries, played with the Oilers 1966–68. Namath, whose career was also hampered by injuries, played with the Jets (1965–76) and the Rams (1977).

34. Passing Fancy/Fancy Passing

Which quarterback led the NFL in passing in 1983?

a. Steve Bartkowski, Falcons
b. Dan Fouts, Chargers
c. Joe Montana, 49ers
d. John Elway, Broncos
e. Danny White, Cowboys
f. Jim Zorn, Seahawks

35. As He Saw Them

Who is the former tackle from Syracuse, drafted number three by the Lions in 1959, who became a major league baseball umpire when a knee injury ended his football career?

a. Nestor Chylak
b. Cal Hubbard
c. Jim Nance
d. Ron Luciano
e. Norm Sherry
f. Earl Weaver

36. Being There

Name the only man at the NFL's organizational meeting in Canton, Ohio, in 1920 who was associated with the NFL until 1983.

   a. George Blanda
   b. Paul Brown
   c. George Halas
   d. Art Rooney
   e. Pete Rozelle
   f. Norm Schachter

37. Mr. Consistency

True or False? Oilers running back Earl Campbell has led the NFL in rushing each year since he came into the league in 1978.

All in the Family

For many years it was generally thought that the first son of an NFL player to play in the NFL was Joe Walton, a tight end with the Redskins in 1957 and the son of Frank (Tiger) Walton (who played with the Redskins in 1934). Research done at the Pro Football Hall of Fame reveals that the Harold Bradleys were the first NFL father-son combination. Harold Sr. played with the Chicago Cardinals in 1928, Harold Jr. with the Browns in 1954.

38. A Chip Off the Old Blocking Dummy

Which of the players listed below is *not* the son of a former NFL player?

    a. Brad Budde, guard, Chiefs
    b. John Hannah, guard, Patriots
    c. Bert Jones, quarterback, Rams
    d. Jeff Kemp, quarterback, Rams
    e. Greg Landry, quarterback, Colts
    f. Billy Cannon, linebacker, Cowboys

39. Camping Out

How wide is the official NFL playing field?

    a. 50 yards
    b. 150 feet
    c. 53⅓ yards
    d. 60 yards
    e. 200 feet
    f. 100 yards

40. Guys of Texas, Part II

Match the NFL defensive players below with the Texas college they attended.

1.	Jacob Green, DE, Seahawks	a.	Texas
2.	Doug English, DT, Lions	b.	Texas
3.	Louie Kelcher, DT, 49ers	c.	Angelo State
4.	Ken Sims, DE, Patriots	d.	Texas A&M
5.	Clayton Weishuhn, LB, Patriots	e.	Texas A&M
6.	Mike Singletary, LB, Bears	f.	Baylor
7.	Thomas Howard, LB, Chiefs	g.	Texas
8.	Ted Watts, CB, Raiders	h.	SMU
9.	Lester Hayes, CB, Raiders	i.	Texas
10.	Johnnie Johnson, S, Rams	j.	Texas
11.	Glenn Blackwood, S, Dolphins	k.	Texas Tech
12.	Raul Allegre, K, Colts	l.	Texas Tech

41. Roaring Twenties

Which is the only team below that did *not* play in the NFL in the 1920s?

a. Decatur, Illinois, Staleys
b. Evansville, Indiana, Crimson Giants
c. Frankford, Pennsylvania, Yellowjackets
d. Muncie, Indiana, Flyers
e. Providence, Rhode Island, Steamroller
f. Springfield, Illinois, Rifles

Odd Man Out

On August 12, 1950, the New York Giants played a preseason game with the Ottawa Rough Riders of the Canadian Football League. One half of the game was played by Canadian rules and one half by NFL rules. What did the Giants do to alter their offense when they had to use the twelfth man? Dick Hensley, an end for the Giants that day, says, "Simple. We just sent a man in motion toward the far sideline and went eleven against eleven with them at the middle of the field." The Giants won the game 27–6.

42. Brown University (of Coaching)

Which NFL head coach is the only one not associated (as player or assistant) with Pro Football Hall of Fame coach Paul Brown?

- a. Monte Clark, Lions
- b. Bud Grant, Vikings
- c. Walt Michaels, Jets
- d. Chuck Noll, Steelers
- e. Don Shula, Dolphins
- f. Bill Walsh, 49ers

43. Versatile

Although he is a member of the Pro Football Hall of Fame as defensive back, he is in the NFL record book for being the receiver on a 98-yard pass play. Who is he?

  a. Jack Butler, Steelers
  b. Jack Christiansen, Lions
  c. Marshall Goldberg, Chicago Cardinals
  d. Dick (Night Train) Lane, Chicago Cardinals
  e. Yale Lary, Lions
  f. Emlen Tunnell, Giants

44. Worth the Wait

Which is the last AFC team to finally qualify for a postseason game?

  a. Cleveland Browns
  b. Cincinnati Bengals
  c. Houston Oilers
  d. New York Jets
  e. Oakland Raiders
  f. Seattle Seahawks

45. Anticipation

Which is the only NFL team that has never played in a postseason game?

    a. Atlanta Falcons
    b. Chicago Bears
    c. New Orleans Saints
    d. New York Giants
    e. St. Louis Cardinals
    f. Tampa Bay Buccaneers

Heavy Hitters

Of the Steelers' defenders who started Super Bowls IX and X, only Ernie Holmes was never selected to play in a Pro Bowl of that era. The Steel Curtain defense included:

Le—L.C. Greenwood
LT—Joe Greene
RT—Ernie Holmes
RE—Dwight White
LLB—Jack Ham
MLB—Jack Lambert
RLB—Andy Russell
LCB—J.T. Thomas
RCB—Mel Blount
SS—Mike Wagner
FS—Glen Edwards

46. Square One

Who coached the Oakland Raiders during their first season (1960)?

    a. Al Davis
    b. Eddie Erdelatz
    c. Frank Leahy
    d. John Madden
    e. John Rauch
    f. Glenn (Pop) Warner

47. Did They Kick the Tires?

The NFL was organized in 1920 in Ralph Hay's Canton, Ohio auto showroom. What type of agency did Hay own?

    a. Chevrolet
    b. Franklin/Nash
    c. Hudson/Willys
    d. Jordan/Hupmobile
    e. Studebaker
    f. Toyota

48. Under Fire

Which former NFL head coach served in combat during the Vietnam War?

- a. Rocky Bleier
- b. Dan Henning
- c. Les Steckel
- d. Joe Gibbs
- e. Ron Meyer
- f. Ralph Houk

49. Canadian Connection

Which of the NFL head coaches below never was associated with the Canadian Football League?

- a. Kay Stephenson, Bills
- b. Bud Grant, Vikings
- c. Forrest Gregg, Packers
- d. Frank Kush, Colts
- e. Hugh Campbell, Oilers
- f. Jim Hanifan, Cardinals

It's In the Cards

The first set of bubble gum cards featuring NFL players was produced by the National Chicle Company in 1934. The player shown on card number one of the first set is Pro Football Hall of Fame quarterback Earl (Dutch) Clark of the Lions.

50. The Other League

Which of the following Pro Football Hall of Fame enshrinees was not primarily associated with the American Football League?

    a. Lance Alworth, flanker
    b. George Blanda, quarterback and kicker
    c. Lamar Hunt, founder and owner
    d. Ron Mix, tackle
    e. Jim Otto, center
    f. Larry Wilson, safety

51. The University of Where?

Match the NFL players below with the colleges they attended.

1.	Lyle Alzado, DE, Raiders	a.	Milton
2.	Ken Anderson, QB, Bengals	b.	Henderson St.
3.	Joe Fields, C, Jets	c.	Augustana
4.	Scott Brunner, QB, Broncos	d.	Widener
5.	Boyce Green, RB, Browns	e.	West Chester State
6.	Dave Jennings, P, Giants	f.	St. Lawrence
7.	Dave Krieg, QB, Seahawks	g.	Wooster
8.	Roy Green, WR, Cardinals	h.	Delaware
9.	Blake Moore, C, Bengals	i.	Carson-Newman
10.	Joe Senser, TE, Vikings	j.	Yankton

52. Charging Ahead

Which of the NFL head coaches below was not a Chargers assistant at one time?

a. Chuck Knox, Seahawks
b. Forrest Gregg, Packers
c. Jim Hanifan, Cardinals
d. Chuck Noll, Steelers
e. Bum Phillips, Saints
f. Bill Walsh, 49ers

53. Two-by-Fours

Name the last two head coaches to have won four or more NFL/Super Bowl championships.

a. George Allen, Redskins, and Don Shula, Dolphins
b. Paul Brown, Browns, and George Halas, Bears
c. George Halas, Bears, and Allie Sherman, Giants
d. Tom Landry, Cowboys, and Chuck Noll, Steelers
e. Tom Landry, Cowboys, and Vince Lombardi, Packers
f. Vince Lombardi, Packers, and Chuck Noll, Steelers

Does J.R. Know About This?

The ranch home of Cloyce Box, a receiver in the NFL from 1940 to 1954 (Redskins and Lions), was used as the original South Fork estate in the television show Dallas.

54. A Popular Fellow

Who was the first draft choice ever of the Kansas City Chiefs, back when they were the Dallas Texans?

a. Billy Cannon
b. Don Meredith
c. Bob Lilly
d. E.J. Holub
e. Ronnie Bull
f. Abner Haynes

55. Running Machine

Which NFL running back gained more than 100 yards in 58 of the 118 games he played?

a. Jim Brown, Browns
b. Earl Campbell, Oilers
c. Tony Dorsett, Cowboys
d. Franco Harris, Steelers
e. Walter Payton, Bears
f. O.J. Simpson, Bills

56. Cornerstone

Who was rookie head coach Chuck Noll's first Steelers draft choice in 1969?

a. Terry Bradshaw, quarterback, Louisiana Tech
b. Joe Greene, defensive tackle, North Texas State
c. Jack Ham, linebacker, Penn State
e. Franco Harris, running back, Penn State
f. John Kolb, center, Oklahoma State
g. Andy Russell, linebacker, Missouri

57. Hot Hands

True or False? In 1981, for the second straight year, three Chargers receivers each gained more than 1,000 yards on pass receptions.

Revolving Door II

In their first year in the NFL (1976), the Tampa Bay Buccaneers had 170 different players on their roster—including 70 during the regular season. The player limit in 1976 was 43.

58. We All Can't Be Perfect

In 1980, only one field goal was missed from within 20 yards. Which NFL kicker holds the dubious distinction of blowing that kick?

a. Chris Bahr, Raiders
b. Matt Bahr, Steelers
c. Ed Murray, Lions
d. Benny Ricardo, Saints
e. John Smith, Patriots
f. Sandro Vitiello, Bengals

59. Dynamic Duo

What was the last year that the AFC/NFC or AFL/NFL pass-catching leaders *each* gained more than 1,000 yards on receptions?

    a. 1984
    b. 1978
    c. 1972
    d. 1981
    e. 1968
    f. 1964

60. Sideline Superintendent

In 1984, which former NFL player was the youngest full-time assistant coach in the NFL?

    a. Tony Dungy, Steelers
    b. Dick Hoak, Steelers
    c. Pat Hodgson, Giants
    d. Rich Kotite, Browns
    e. Kay Stephenson, Bills
    f. David Shula, Dolphins

61. Three for Three for Three

Name the running back whose statistics for a 1979 game read: three attempts, three yards, three touchdowns.

    a. Scott Dierking, Jets
    b. Clarence Harmon, Redskins
    c. Scott Laidlaw, Cowboys
    d. Walter Payton, Bears
    e. Booker Russell, Raiders
    f. Sidney Thornton, Steelers

No Harm, No Foul

The Brooklyn Dodgers were not a very successful NFL franchise (1930–1944), but they are in the NFL record book twice for playing in a game in which there were no penalties assessed: against Pittsburgh in 1934, and against Boston in 1936.

62. Getting Good Mileage

Which NFL quarterback became the first to attempt more than 600 passes in a season and average 300 yards passing a game?

    a. Steve Bartkowski, Falcons
    b. Lynn Dickey, Packers
    c. Dan Fouts, Chargers
    d. Craig Morton, Broncos
    e. Brian Sipe, Browns
    f. David Woodley, Dolphins

63. Javelin Catcher Supreme

Which NFL kick returner set a record in 1981 by compiling 207 yards on six punt returns in one game?

    a. James Brooks, Chargers
    b. Jeff Groth, Saints
    c. LeRoy Irvin, Rams
    d. Carl Roaches, Oilers
    e. Freddie Solomon, 49ers
    f. Scott Woerner, Falcons

64. A Grand Total

In 1983 there were more 1,000-yard rushers in the NFL than ever before. How many were there?
    a. 9
    b. 11
    c. 13
    d. 16
    e. 17
    f. 18

65. They Could Have Caught the Kitchen Sink, Too

True or False? Charley Hennigan of the Oilers and Lionel Taylor of the Broncos are the only two receivers to make 100 or more receptions in a season.

Taking Their Membership Seriously

Each NFL running back who gains 1,000 yards or more in a single season is granted membership in the somewhat mythical 1,000-Yard Club. Three runners have met the requirements literally: Willie Ellison of the Rams (1971), Mercury Morris of the Dolphins (1972), and Greg Pruitt of the Browns (1976). Each gained exactly 1,000 yards.

66. The Lone Ranger

Of the NFL head coaches below, who is the only one to play in the NFL?

    a. John Robinson, Rams
    b. Don Coryell, Chargers
    c. Dan Henning, Falcons
    d. Jim Hanifan, Cardinals
    e. Leeman Bennett, Buccaneers
    f. Hugh Campbell, Oilers

67. Maybe He Knew Better

Of the NFL head coaches below, which is the only one who did *not* play in the NFL?

    a. Forrest Gregg, Packers
    b. Joe Walton, Jets
    c. Chuck Noll, Steelers
    d. Kay Stephenson, Bills
    e. Bum Phillips, Saints
    f. Don Shula, Dolphins

68. Running Away With It

Which of the NFL running backs below is the only one *not* to have gained 200 or more yards in one game?

- a. Earl Campbell, Oilers, 1980
- b. Tony Dorsett, Cowboys, 1977
- c. Chuck Foreman, Vikings, 1976
- d. Franco Harris, Steelers, 1977
- e. Terry Miller, Bills, 1978
- f. O.J. Simpson, Bills, 1976

69. "A" for Accuracy

Which qualifying NFL quarterback, although ninth in overall passing ratings, led the league in completion percentage in 1983?

- a. Terry Bradshaw, Steelers
- b. Dan Fouts, Chargers
- c. Ken Anderson, Bengals
- d. Joe Theismann, Redskins
- e. David Woodley, Dolphins
- f. Jim Zorn, Seahawks

Closed Circuit Coach

In 1950, coach Dick Gallagher of Santa Clara was hospitalized. He directed his team from his sickbed. By rigging up a television set and a telephone to the Stanford Stadium sidelines in Palo Alto, California, Gallagher was able to communicate with his Broncos staff and players. Although he could not call every play, Gallagher, who later was an assistant coach with the Browns, general manager of the Bills, and director of the Pro Football Hall of Fame, was able to make many valuable suggestions. However, the final score read: Stanford 23, Santa Clara 13.

70. They Did Okay Otherwise

Which of the well-known running backs below is the only one to gain more than 1,000 yards in a season?

   a. Cliff Battles
   b. Tony Canadeo
   c. Bill Dudley
   d. Ollie Matson
   e. Hugh McElhenny
   f. Bronko Nagurski

71. Not Bad for Openers

Which free agent rookie defensive back led the NFL in interceptions in 1981?

  a. Louis Breeden, Bengals
  b. Kenny Easley, Seahawks
  c. Michael Downs, Cowboys
  d. John Harris, Seahawks
  e. Ronnie Lott, 49ers
  f. Everson Walls, Cowboys

72. This Old House

Which is the oldest stadium in the NFL?

  a. Cleveland Stadium, Cleveland
  b. Lambeau Field, Green Bay
  c. Veterans Stadium, Philadelphia
  d. Pontiac Silverdome, Detroit
  e. Orange Bowl, Miami
  f. Soldier Field, Chicago

73. Wet Paint

Which is the newest stadium in the NFL?

  a. Astrodome, Houston
  b. Hubert H. Humphrey Metrodome, Minneapolis
  c. Kingdome, Seattle
  d. Pontiac Silverdome, Detroit
  e. Rich Stadium, Buffalo
  f. Texas Stadium, Dallas

Patented Kicker

Fred Cox, who established an NFL record by scoring in 151 consecutive games while playing for the Vikings (1963–73), holds the patent on the Nerf Ball—the soft, spongy football kids can't throw through windows.

74. Fake It Till You Make It

In 1946, the Boston Yanks did not make a field goal all season. How many did that defunct NFL team attempt?

    a. 0
    b. 1
    c. 2
    d. 6
    e. 9
    f. 13

75. When in Doubt, Hand Off

Which running back set an NFL record for most rushing attempts with 407 carries in 1984?

    a. Earl Campbell, Oilers
    b. George Rogers, Saints
    c. Tony Dorsett, Cowboys
    d. Eric Dickerson, Rams
    e. Wilbert Montgomery, Eagles
    f. James Wilder, Buccaneers

76. That's Durable Spelled with Two O's

True or False? Pro Football Hall of Fame center Jim Otto started every game for the Raiders during their entire AFL tenure, 1960–69.

77. Global Affairs

Which team was not a member of the defunct World Football League in 1974 or 1975?

- a. Birmingham Vulcans
- b. Chicago Sting
- c. Detroit Wheels
- d. Jacksonville Express
- e. Portland Storm
- f. Southern California Sun

Where Have You Gone, Providence Steamroller?

Before the NFL realigned in 1970 and expanded to its present 28 teams in 1976, the highest number of teams was 22 in 1926. The lowest total was 8 teams in 1932 and 1943. In 1943, Cleveland suspended operations for a year, and Pittsburgh and Philadelphia merged to form the "Steagles."

78. Under(class) Achievers

Which NFL player did not win the Heisman Trophy as a college junior?

    a. Tony Dorsett, running back, Cowboys—1975, Pittsburgh
    b. Archie Griffin, running back, Bengals—1974, Ohio State
    c. Vic Janowicz, halfback, Redskins—1950, Ohio State
    d. Billy Sims, running back, Lions—1978, Oklahoma
    e. Roger Staubach, quarterback, Cowboys—1963, Navy
    f. Doak Walker, halfback, Lions—1948, Southern Methodist

79. Pumping Iron

One of the strongest men ever in the NFL, he has bench-pressed 585 pounds. Who is he?

    a. Cullen Bryant, running back, Seahawks
    b. Lawrence Taylor, linebacker, Giants
    c. Mike Webster, center, Steelers
    d. Dwight Stephenson, center, Dolphins
    e. Steve Watson, wide receiver, Denver
    f. Ed White, guard, Chargers

80. Not a Bad Average

Which NFL running back was the first player in history to gain a total of more than 3,000 yards in his first two professional seasons?

- a. Ottis Anderson, Cardinals
- b. Earl Campbell, Oilers
- c. Tony Dorsett, Cowboys
- d. Franco Harris, Steelers
- e. Walter Payton, Bears
- f. O.J. Simpson, Bills

81. Out in the Open

Which receiver became the tenth player in the NFL to make more than 500 career receptions? He did it in 1981.

- a. Jerry Butler, wide receiver, Bills
- b. Harold Carmichael, wide receiver, Eagles
- c. John Stallworth, wide receiver, Steelers
- d. Lynn Swann, wide receiver, Steelers
- e. Pat Tilley, wide receiver, Cardinals
- f. Kellen Winslow, tight end, Chargers

Padded Prices

A 1909 copy of the Sears & Roebuck Catalog lists prices for various pieces of football equipment. Below is a comparison with today's prices.

	1909	Today
Helmet	$1.10	$98.00
Nose guard/facemask	.70	13.50
Jacket/jersey	.37	65.00
Pants	.58	50.00
Shin guards	.35	11.00
Shoes	1.85	39.95
Football	3.20	42.50

Note: The 1909 catalog did not offer shoulder pads or hip pads. Quilting was sewn into the football "jacket" (jersey) and pants in place of separate pads.

82. The House That Ruth Built

Which modern-day NFL team was the first to play in Yankee Stadium?

a. Boston Yanks, 1945
b. New York Bulldogs, 1949
c. New York Yanks, 1950
d. New York Giants, 1956
e. New York Titans, 1960
f. New York Jets, 1965

83. The Old One-Two

Which NFL defender intercepted just two passes in 1980 and returned both of them for touchdowns?

   a. Louis Breeden, cornerback, Bengals
   b. Randy Gradishar, linebacker, Broncos
   c. Ray Griffin, cornerback, Bengals
   d. Kurt Knoff, safety, Vikings
   e. Jack Youngblood, defensive end, Rams
   f. Jim Youngblood, linebacker, Rams

84. The Penguin and Bobby Moore

True or False? Vikings wide receiver Ahmad Rashad and Los Angeles Dodgers third baseman Ron Cey were members of the same high school backfield.

85. These Hallowed Halls

Which of the players below is *not* a member of the Pro Football Hall of Fame?

   a. Doug Atkins, defensive end, Browns, Bears, and Saints
   b. Sam Huff, linebacker, Giants and Redskins
   c. George Musso, guard-tackle, Bears
   d. Merlin Olsen, defensive tackle, Rams
   e. Don Perkins, running back, Cowboys
   f. Jim Taylor, running back, Packers and Saints

When mentioned in The First Official NFL Trivia Book, *Tom Pridemore was noted for his unusual offensive occupation, a page for the West Virginia State Legislature. Since then, he's successfully run for a seat in the State's House of Delegates. At age 26, the Atlanta safety is state's youngest lawmaker. Speaking of successfully running, Pridemore returned an interception 101 yards for a touchdown during the 1981 season.*

86. Familiar Territory

The first three 1984 draft choices for the Altanta Falcons were all from the same college. Name the school.

   a. Oklahoma
   b. USC
   c. Penn State
   d. Notre Dame
   e. Arizona State
   f. Susquehanna

87. Quite a Guy

Although he was an outstanding punter and placekicker in college, the Raiders' Ray Guy also excelled at another position. What else did he play at Southern Mississippi?

   a. Cornerback
   b. Defensive tackle
   c. Running back
   d. Quarterback
   e. Safety
   f. Wide receiver

88. The Original Sugarland Express

Ken Hall, who played briefly with the Cardinals and Oilers (1959–61), holds a record that may never be broken. How many rushing yards did he amass in his four years at Sugarland, Texas, High School?

    a. 4,045
    b. 6,008
    c. 8,724
    d. 9,003
    e. 11,121
    f. 13,333

89. They Really Were GIANTS

Which of the following members of the New York Giants of the 1950s and 1960s has *not* been elected to the Pro Football Hall of Fame?

    a. Roosevelt Brown, tackle
    b. Charlie Conerly, quarterback
    c. Frank Gifford, halfback
    d. Sam Huff, linebacker
    e. Andy Robustelli, defensive end
    f. Emlen Tunnell, safety

Slow But Sure

Dallas's Tony Dorsett has rushed for more than 1,000 yards seven different times in the NFL. Before he became the Cowboys' career rushing leader, the old team record holder—Don Perkins—had never gained as much as 1,000 in a season even once. Dorsett's total fell to 745 in the nine-game 1982 season. He rushed for 1,320 yards in 1983.

90. In a Class by Himself

In 1983, Steelers running back Franco Harris set a record for the most 1,000-yard rushing seasons. How many years did he surpass that mark?

   a. 12
   b. 6
   c. 13
   d. 10
   e. 8
   f. 9

91. Permanent Fixture

Which NFL star played in a record 14 Pro Bowls during his 15-year career?

   a. Jim Brown, running back, Browns
   b. Joe Greene, defensive tackle, Steelers
   c. Ken Houston, safety, Oilers, Redskins
   d. Gino Marchetti, defensive end, Colts
   e. Leo Nomellini, defensive tackle, 49ers
   f. Merlin Olsen, defensive tackle, Rams

92. Starr of the Show

Bart Starr of the Packers holds the record for most passing attempts without an interception. What is his record?

   a. 137
   b. 208
   c. 294
   d. 311
   e. 333
   f. 502

93. Like Kissing Your Sister

Which NFL team holds the record for the most tie games (6) in a season?

    a. Frankford Yellowjackets, 1929
    b. Chicago Bears, 1932
    c. Chicago Bears, 1940
    d. New York Giants, 1943
    e. New York Giants, 1957
    f. Minnesota Vikings, 1980

Perennial All-Star

Because of manpower problems during World War II, Charley Trippi of Georgia played in four Chicago All-Star games, 1943–45 and 1947, with the stars. As a member of the NFL champion Chicago Cardinals, Trippi again played in the Chicago game in 1948. Trippi, who played with the Cardinals from 1947 through 1955, was elected to the Pro Football Hall of Fame in 1968.

94. Getting a Handle on Things

In 1980, which NFL team tied the 1938 Philadelphia Eagles for the record of fewest fumbles lost in a season?

    a. Cowboys
    b. Dolphins
    c. Jets
    d. Patriots
    e. Rams
    f. Vikings

95. Scoring Big

Which NFL running back set a record by scoring 24 rushing touchdowns in 1983?

    a. George Rogers, Saints
    b. Eric Dickerson, Rams
    c. John Riggins, Redskins
    d. Billy Sims, Lions
    e. Wendell Tyler, 49ers
    f. Steve Watson, Broncos

96. Fast Company

Which quarterback moved to third place on the all-time NFL passing yardage list in 1983?

    a. Terry Bradshaw
    b. Jim Hart
    c. Ron Jaworski
    d. Craig Morton
    e. Ken Stabler
    f. Jim Zorn

97. All in the Family

Name the NFL lineman who is married to the daughter of Pro Football Hall of Fame running back Jim Brown?

    a. Irv Pankey, tackle, Rams
    b. Morris Towns, tackle, Oilers
    c. Ed Jones, defensive end, Cowboys
    d. Marvin Powell, tackle, Jets
    e. Herbert Scott, guard, Cowboys
    f. Chris Ward, tackle, Saints

98. Legal Bengal

Which Cincinnati player has a law degree?

    a. Ken Anderson, quarterback
    b. Pat McInally, punter
    c. Isaac Curtis, wide receiver
    d. Guy Frazier, linebacker
    e. Ray Horton, cornerback
    f. Turk Schonert, quarterback

99. Giving Good Measure

In 1980, an NFL wide receiver made only three catches, but all were for touchdowns. Who was he?

    a. Dwight Clark, 49ers
    b. Johnny (Lam) Jones, Jets
    c. Steve Kreider, Bengals
    d. Haven Moses, Broncos
    e. Jim Smith, Steelers
    f. Keith Wright, Browns

The Reeves Legacy

The following persons were protégés of Daniel F. Reeves, owner of the Rams (1943–71).

NAME	RAMS POSITION	OTHER POSITION(S)
Bill Granholm	Equipment manager (1949–67)	*Special assistant to the NFL Commissioner (1967–1983), assistant to the president, NFC (1983 to date)*
Elroy (Crazylegs) Hirsch	Offensive end (1949–57) General manager (1960–62) Assistant to the president (1963–68)	*Athletic director, University of Wisconsin (1969 to date)*
Kay Lang	Ticket department assistant and secretary to the business manager (1946–59)	*Ticket manager, Dallas Cowboys (1960–84)*
Tex Maule	Assistant public relations director (1949–52)	*Public relations director, Dallas Texans (1952)* *Pro football writer for several magazines, including Sports Illustrated (1956–79)*
Bert Rose	Public relations director (1955–60)	*General manager, Minnesota Vikings (1961), vice president, Texas Stadium Corporation (1969 to date)*

Pete Rozelle	Public relations director (1952–55) General manager (1957–59)	NFL Commissioner (1960 to date)
Johnny Sanders	Scout (1952–64) Director of player personnel (1964–69), Assistant general manager (1969–75)	General manager, San Diego Chargers (1975 to date)
Tex Schramm	Public relations director (1947–52), Assistant to the president (1952–55), General manager (1955–57)	Assistant director, CBS Sports 1957–60), president and general manager, Dallas Cowboys (1960 to date)
Jack Teele	Public relations director (1960–69), assistant to the president (1969–71), administrative assistant to the owner (1972–78), vice president, administration (1972–81)	Assistant to the president, San Diego Chargers (1981 to date)
Paul (Tank) Younger	Fullback (1949–57), Scout (1958–75)	Assistant general manager, San Diego Chargers (1975 to date)

100. Best Foot Forward

True or False? Ed Murray (Lions) is the only kicker to be named most valuable player in the AFC-NFC Pro Bowl.

101. Room for Improvement

Which NFL team never has finished a season with a winning record?

    a. Houston Oilers
    b. Chicago Bears
    c. New Orleans Saints
    d. Pittsburgh Steelers
    e. St. Louis Cardinals
    f. Seattle Seahawks

102. It's So Hard to Find Good Help

The Cleveland Browns used three placekickers at various times in 1981 (Dave Jacobs, Steve Cox, and Matt Bahr). How many kickers did they have between their inception in 1946 and 1981?

    a. 1
    b. 3
    c. 5
    d. 9
    e. 23
    f. 36

During the 1981 season, the Raiders were shut out three successive weeks (16–0 by Detroit, 17–0 by Denver, and 27–0 by Kansas City). While somewhat embarrassing, it wasn't an NFL record. That "honor" still belongs to the Brooklyn Dodgers, who were whitewashed in their final two games of the 1942 season and the first four of 1943.

103. The Bronze Age

True or False? The Lions and the Rams have each had six Heisman Trophy winners on their teams.

104. 2,003

O.J. Simpson (Bills and 49ers) was the first running back in NFL history to gain more than 2,000 yards in one season. Before Eric Dickerson broke his record in 1984, which NFL running back had come closest to that total?

    a. Jim Brown
    b. Earl Campbell
    c. Tony Dorsett
    d. Franco Harris
    e. Walter Payton
    f. George Rogers

105. Triple Dipper

Which NFL player was selected to the Pro Bowl for three consecutive years with three different teams—New York Yanks 1951, Dallas Texans 1952, and Baltimore Colts 1953?

    a. Alan Ameche, fullback
    b. Lenny Moore, flanker
    c. Chet Mutryn, halfback
    d. Orban (Spec) Sanders, halfback
    e. George Taliaferro, halfback
    f. Buddy Young, halfback

106. A Good Season That Day

True or False? The 18 passes Tom Fears of the Rams caught in one game (December 3, 1950, against Green Bay) for an NFL record would have led the NFL for the entire season in 1934.

Indianapolis Triangles?

There's a case to be made that the roots of the present Indianapolis Colts franchise go back to the Dayton, Ohio, Triangles—an original NFL team. The Triangles, who played in the NFL from 1920 to 1929, transferred their franchise to Brooklyn for the 1930 season. The Dodgers played in the NFL until 1944, when they changed their name to the Brooklyn Tigers. (Are you with us so far?) The Tigers merged with the Boston Yanks for the 1945 season. The Yanks moved to New York in 1949 and played as the Bulldogs. Meanwhile, the Colts folded in Baltimore after the 1950 season, and sent a strong nucleus of their players to join the New York Yanks (the Bulldogs had changed their name for 1950 season) in 1951. The Yanks folded, sending many of their players to the newly formed Dallas Texans in 1952. The Texans turned their franchise back to the league during the 1952 season. In 1953 Baltimore was awarded a franchise that included many of the Yanks' and Texans' key players. The Colts were in Baltimore from 1953 until moving to Indianapolis in the spring of 1984.

107. Kiss It Goodbye

Which member of the Pro Football Hall of Fame gave up two home runs to Babe Ruth the year he hit 60 (1927)?

    a. Morris (Red) Badgro
    b. Earl (Dutch) Clark
    c. Ernie Nevers
    d. Joe Perry
    e. Jim Thorpe
    f. Bob Waterfield

108. A Young Turk

Which player is the only native of Istanbul, Turkey, to play in the NFL?

a. Ken Bordelon, linebacker, Saints
b. Ken Calicutt, running back, Lions
c. Tunch Ilkin, guard-tackle, Steelers
d. Ahmad Rashad, wide receiver, Vikings
e. Rafael Septien, kicker, Cowboys
f. Godwin Turk, linebacker, Broncos

109. Hitting the Open Man

Which NFL quarterback holds a record for having eight passes intercepted in one game?

a. Parker Hall, Cleveland Rams, 1942
b. Jim Hardy, Chicago Cardinals, 1950
c. Frank Sinkwich, Detroit Lions, 1943
d. Ken Stabler, Oakland Raiders, 1977
e. Tommy Wade, Pittsburgh Steelers, 1965
f. Bob Waterfield, Los Angeles Rams, 1948

110. How Could They Forget What's-His-Name?

It is generally thought that the Cowboys have had only three
middle linebackers in the team's history—Jerry Tubbs, Lee
Roy Jordan,and Bob Breunig. However, a fourth man played
the position for part of the 1960 season. Who is he?

   a. Monte Clark
   b. Bud Grant
   c. Ray Malavasi
   d. Walt Michaels
   e. Chuck Noll
   f. Jack Patera

Celluloid Heroes

*A partial list of NFL players who have appeared in feature
films:*

1. *Doug Atkins*, Heartbreak Pass
2. *Jim Brown*, The Dirty Dozen
3. *Larry Csonka*, Midway
4. *Arthur (Hec) Garvey*, The Quarterback
5. *Elroy (Crazylegs) Hirsch*, Unchained
6. *Ed (Too Tall) Jones*, Squeeze Play
7. *Joe Klecko*, Smokey and the Bandit, II
8. *Ray Mansfield*, S-h-h-h-h
9. *John Matuszak*, North Dallas Forty
10. *Merlin Olsen*, The Undefeated
11. *Paul Robeson*, The Emperor Jones
12. *Tim Rossovich*, The Long Riders
13. *Joe Theismann*, The Man with Bogart's Face
14. *Carl Weathers*, Rocky
15. *Tom Woodeschik*, M*A*S*H

111. He's a Three-Letter Man

Atlanta safety Bob Glazebrook has an unusual nickname.
Which is it?

   a. AAA
   b. BMW
   c. IBM
   d. ITT
   e. KGB
   f. TWX

112. Mr. Longshot

Which NFL kicker holds the field goal distance record in both
Super Bowl and Pro Bowl competition?

   a. Don Chandler
   b. Roy Gerela
   c. Efren Herrera
   d. Mark Moseley
   e. Jan Stenerud
   f. Garo Yepremian

113. One If By Land . . .

In the 1920s, when the New York Giants played the Providence, Rhode Island, Steamroller, they used an unconventional method of travel. Which mode of transportation did the team use?

    a. airplane
    b. boat
    c. stagecoach
    d. subway
    e. train
    f. water taxi

114. Clean Sweep

In the first year of the American Football League (1960), which player was named rookie of the year *and* most valuable player?

    a. Billy Cannon, halfback, Houston Oilers
    b. Cookie Gilchrist, fullback, Buffalo Bills
    c. Abner Haynes, halfback, Dallas Texans
    d. Paul Lowe, halfback, Los Angeles Chargers
    e. Dave Smith, fullback, Houston Oilers
    f. Charley Tolar, fullback, Houston Oilers

Bengals Balladeer

Mike Reid, an All-American from Penn State, became an all-pro defensive tackle with the Cincinnati Bengals in the 1970s, but left football after just five seasons to pursue a music career. He is now one of the most respected songwriters in Nashville and had his song "Inside"—sung by Ronnie Millsap—hit the top of the Country charts in 1983. Reid also won a Grammy award for writing "Stranger In My House," also recorded by Millsap.

115. It's Saul in the Family

Which NFL assistant coach was affiliated with all the teams for which the Saul brothers—Bill (Steelers), Ron (Redskins), and Rich (Rams)—played?

- a. Bill Austin
- b. Jim Garrett
- c. Bill Muir
- d. Dan Sekanovich
- e. LaVern Torgeson
- f. Walt Yowarsky

116. At Least We Didn't Lose 73–0

The most lopsided game in the NFL was the 1940 championship game, when the Bears defeated the Redskins 73–0. What is the score of the highest regular season shutout?

    a. 55–0
    b. 57–0
    c. 59–0
    d. 64–0
    e. 69–0
    f. 71–0

117. I've Heard of Specialists, But . . .

Which NFL player can claim the longest (101 yards) and the second longest (100) return of a missed field goal attempt?

    a. Mel Blount, cornerback, Steelers
    b. Ken Ellis, cornerback, Packers
    c. Al Nelson, safety, Eagles
    d. Eddie Payton, kick returner, Vikings
    e. O.J. Simpson, running back, Bills
    f. Charlie Waters, safety, Cowboys

118. Space Invader

Who holds the NFL record for most yards receiving for a single game?

    a. Lance Alworth, Chargers, 1966
    b. Jim Benton, Rams, 1945
    c. Charley Hennigan, Oilers, 1961
    d. Don Maynard, Jets, 1968
    e. Johnny Morris, Bears, 1964
    f. Charley Taylor, Redskins, 1974

The People's Choice

Using fans' requests for video tapes, NFL Films has determined the most popular individuals, teams, and games as follows: Individuals: *Jim Brown, Franco Harris, and Roger Staubach.*

Teams: *Green Bay Packers of the 1960s, Dallas Cowboys of the 1970s, and the Pittsburgh Steelers of the 1970s.*

Games: *1958 NFL Championship (Baltimore 23, New York Giants 17 in sudden-death overtime); 1967 NFL Championship (Green Bay 21, Dallas 17 in 13-below-zero weather); and the 1972 AFC Divisional Playoff (Pittsburgh 13, Oakland 7, featuring Franco Harris's "Immaculate Reception").*

119. Double Nickel

Bob Shaw, of the Chicago Cardinals, set an NFL record in 1950 with five touchdown catches in a single game. Who tied his record in 1981?

  a. Jerry Butler, Bills
  b. Roger Carr, Colts
  c. Earnest Gray, Giants
  d. John Stallworth, Steelers
  e. Lynn Swann, Steelers
  f. Kellen Winslow, Chargers

120. Just Kicking Around

Which kicking specialist played in the All-America Football Conference, the National Football League, and the American Football League?

  a. Ben Agajanian
  b. George Blanda
  c. Lou Groza
  d. Booth Lusteg
  e. Gene Mingo
  f. Herb Trevenio

121. Sack Time

Which two teams' defensive units share the single-game record for the most sacks (12) in one game?

a. Colts, 1980, and Steelers, 1966
b. Cowboys, 1981, and 49ers, 1981
c. Lions, 1962, and Bengals, 1980
d. Packers, 1963, and Steelers, 1976
e. Raiders, 1979, and Rams, 1978
f. Redskins, 1942, and Bears, 1937

122. Two Diamonds and a Zircon

Which NFC running back missed the NFL triple crown (rushing, receiving, and scoring championships) when he fell six yards short of the league's highest rushing total?

a. Ottis Anderson, Cardinals, 1980
b. Tony Dorsett, Cowboys, 1981
c. Chuck Foreman, Vikings, 1975
d. Robert Newhouse, Cowboys, 1976
e. Jim Otis, Cardinals, 1974
f. Walter Payton, Bears, 1978

In the mid-1930s, the town of Adel, Iowa (population 1,487) fielded a pretty good American Legion baseball team. The catcher was Adel's all-around athlete Nile Kinnick. The pitcher came from nearby Van Meter (population 358). His name was Bob Feller. Kinnick went on to the University of Iowa, where he won All-America football honors and the Heisman Trophy. Feller signed with the Cleveland Indians and was pitching regularly in the big leagues as a 17-year-old. Despite his size (5 feet 8 inches, 167 pounds), Kinnick was drafted by the NFL's Brooklyn Dodgers. He lost his life in a World War II plane crash and never played pro football.

123. Air Strike

On October 24, 1965, the Cowboys and Packers combined to record the lowest net team passing yardage in a single game. What was the total?

    a. -103 yards
    b. -11 yards
    c. 0 yards
    d. 14 yards
    e. 17 yards
    f. 23 yards

124. Charter Revoked

Which present AFC team was *not* an original AFL franchise?

a. Indianapolis Colts
b. Buffalo Bills
c. Denver Broncos
d. Houston Oilers
e. New England Patriots
f. Los Angeles Raiders

125. Portsiders

In the late 1970s, the Raiders had two left-handed quarterbacks. Who were they?

a. Jim Del Gazio and Ken Stabler
b. David Humm and Ken Stabler
c. Dave Jaynes and Ken Stabler
d. Gifford Nielsen and Ken Stabler
e. Mike Rae and Ken Stabler
f. Marc Wilson and Ken Stabler

126. The Hands Were Familiar

Which quarterback and receiver from the same NFL team combined on the longest AFC-NFC Pro Bowl pass play?

a. Steve Bartkowski and Wallace Francis, Falcons
b. Terry Bradshaw and John Stallworth, Steelers
c. Terry Bradshaw and Lynn Swann, Steelers
d. Jim Hart and Mel Gray, Cardinals
e. Dan Pastorini and Ken Burrough, Oilers
f. Norman Snead and Bob Grim, Giants

Multiple Choices

Since the NFL player draft was instituted in 1936, only five colleges have produced more than two players who were chosen first overall in the yearly selection.

Notre Dame (5): Angelo Bertelli, quarterback, 1944, Boston Yanks; Frank (Boley) Dancewicz, quarterback, 1946, Boston Yanks; Leon Hart, end, 1950, Lions; Paul Hornung, quarterback, 1957, Packers; Walt Patulski, defensive end, 1972, Bills.

Georgia (3): Frank Sinwich, halfback, 1943, Lions; Charley Trippi, halfback, 1945, Chicago Cardinals; Harry Babcock, end, 1953, 49ers.

Stanford (3): Bobby Garrett, quarterback, 1954, Browns; Jim Plunkett, quarterback, 1971, Patriots; John Elway, quarterback, 1983, Colts.

Texas (3): Tommy Nobis, linebacker, 1966, Falcons; Earl Campbell, running back, 1978, Oilers; Ken Sims, defensive tackle, 1982, Patriots.

USC (3): Ron Yary, tackle, 1968, Vikings; O.J. Simpson, running back, 1969, Bills; Ricky Bell, running back, 1977, Buccaneers.

127. Members Only

True or False? During the 1979 season, the Steelers did not have one man on their roster who had spent time with another NFL team.

128. Both Heavy Hitters

One brother was a 1,000-yard rusher in the NFL, the other led the American League (baseball) in batting. Name this brother act.

  a. John and Lou Brockington
  b. Ron and Alex Johnson
  c. Alex and Lou Karras
  d. Leroy and Pat Kelly
  e. Jackie and Paul Robinson
  f. Bubba and Tody Smith

129. Almost There

Which NFL Lineman placed second in the Heisman Trophy voting in 1957?

  a. Dan Currie, center, Michigan State
  b. Lou Cardileone, tackle, Clemson
  c. Jim Houston, guard, Ohio State
  d. Alex Karras, tackle, Iowa
  e. Jerry Kramer, guard, Idaho
  f. Bob Reifsnyder, tackle, Navy

130. Wanna Lift?

Many NFL teams have a strength coach, but who first filled such a position on a full-time basis?
- a. Ray Abernathy, Chiefs, 1972
- b. Clyde Evans, Rams, 1974
- c. Bob Mischak, Raiders, 1965
- d. Lou Riecke, Steelers, 1969
- e. Alvin Roy, Chargers, 1963
- f. Bob Ward, Cowboys, 1966

131. Favorite Son

Which former NFL player has a town or city named in his honor?

- a. Dallas Hickman
- b. Ken Houston
- c. Henry Lawrence
- d. Elijah Pitts
- e. Jim Thorpe
- f. Woody Woodbury

They Also Serve . . .

On September 23, 1945, two of the most powerful service football teams—the Fleet City Bluejackets and the Second Air Force Superbombers—met. Fleet City defeated the Second Air Force, 7–0. Below are some of the players.

Name	Position	Team	NFL team
Dick Barwegan	guard	Second Air Force	Colts and Bears
Paul Christman	quarterback	Fleet City	Cardinals
Tom Fears*	end	Second Air Force	Rams
Val Jansante	end	Fleet City	Steelers
Frank (Bruiser) Kinard*	tackle	Fleet City	Dodgers
Frank Sinkwich	halfback	Second Air Force	Lions
Clyde (Bulldog) Turner*	center	Second Air Force	Bears
Buddy Young	halfback	Fleet City	Yanks and Colts

*Members of the Pro Football Hall of Fame

132. Give Him an Inch . . .

In 1943, which running back missed leading the NFL in rushing by one yard?

    a. Bill Dudley, Detroit Lions
    b. Fred Gehrke, Cleveland Rams
    c. Jack Hinkle, Phil-Pitt "Steagles"
    d. Bill Paschal, New York Giants
    e. Byron (Whizzer) White, Detroit Lions
    f. Joe Zeno, Boston Yanks

133. Air Aces

True or False? In the 1981 AFC Divisional Playoff Game (Dolphins vs. Chargers), Don Strock of the Dolphins and Dan Fouts of the Chargers each passed for more than 400 yards.

134. Off Broadway

Which New York sports figure was known as "Broadway Joe" several years before Joe Namath?

    a. Joe Belinsky
    b. Joe Coleman
    c. Joe DiMaggio
    d. Joe Gordon
    e. Joe Morgan
    f. Joe Pepitone

Never Before, Never Again

Steve Filipowicz, a native of Kulpmont, Pennsylvania, who played college football at Fordham, began 1945 as a reserve catcher for baseball's New York Giants. He finished the year as quarterback-halfback with the New York Giants of the NFL. No one had previously played for both New York Giants teams in the same year, and it is unlikely that anyone will again.

135. Before the Creation

Which Pro Football Hall of Fame coach was an NFL head coach longer than any other man?

a. Paul Brown, Browns and Bengals
b. Weeb Ewbank, Colts and Jets
c. George Halas, Bears
d. Curly Lambeau, Packers, Cardinals, and Redskins
e. Tom Landry, Cowboys
f. Steve Owen, Giants

136. Making His Points

Which versatile performer holds the NFL single-season scoring record by a 15-point margin?

a. Jim Brown, Browns
b. Paul Hornung, Packers
c. Don Hutson, Packers
d. Billy Kilmer, 49ers
e. Lenny Moore, Colts
f. Bob Waterfield, Rams

137. The Inflationary Cost of Spiraling

Today's Wilson official NFL football costs $42.50. What was the cost of a football used in the NFL During the 1920s?

  a. $3.50
  b. $5.00
  c. $9.00
  d. $13.50
  e. $20.00
  f. $37.50

138. Magnetic Personality

Tight end Kellen Winslow of the Chargers set a record by making 13 catches in the 1981 AFC Divisional Playoff against the Dolphins. Which receiver previously held the *postseason* record?

  a. Lance Alworth, Chargers
  b. Raymond Berry, Colts
  c. Tony Nathan, Dolphins
  d. John Stallworth, Steelers
  e. Lynn Swann, Steelers
  f. Warren Wells, Raiders

All-World

The following players first played professional football with the defunct World Football League, 1974–75, and then in the NFL.

PLAYER	POSITION	NFL TEAM & FIRST YEAR	WFL TEAM
Gary Danielson	quarterback	Lions, 1976	Charlotte Hornets
Charles DeJurnett	defensive tackle	Chargers, 1976	Southern California Sun
Pat Haden	quarterback	Rams, 1976	Southern California Sun
Matt Herkenhoff	tackle	Chiefs, 1976	Charlotte Hornets
Alfred Jenkins	wide receiver	Falcons, 1975	Birmingham Americans
Art Kuehn	center	Seahawks, 1976	Southern California Sun
Karl Lorch	defensive end	Redskins, 1976	Hawaiians
Gary Shirk	tight end	Giants, 1976	Memphis Southmen
Greg Stemrick	cornerback	Oilers, 1975	Chicago Fire
Danny White	quarterback, punter	Cowboys, 1976	Memphis Southmen

139. A Spartan Den

The Detroit Lions came into the NFL in 1934. From which Ohio city was the franchise transferred?

a. Akron
b. Canton
c. Cincinnati
d. Columbus
e. Dayton
f. Portsmouth

140. All-American

Which running back had the highest career yards-per-carry average during the 10 years of the American Football League?

a. Emerson Boozer, Jets
b. Clem Daniel, Raiders
c. Cookie Gilchrist, Bills
d. Wendell Hayes, Chiefs
e. Abner Haynes, Chiefs
f. Paul Lowe, Chargers

141. Nothing But Sevens

Which NFL quarterback *never* passed for seven touchdowns in a single game?

a. George Blanda, Oilers, 1961
b. Adrian Burk, Eagles, 1954
c. Joe Kapp, Vikings, 1969
d. Sid Luckman, Bears, 1943
e. Y.A. Tittle, Giants, 1962
f. Johnny Unitas, Colts, 1958

142. New Kid in Town

Which position did *not* exist in the NFL 30 years ago?

a. Flanker
b. Tight end
c. Halfback
d. Middle guard
e. Quarterback
f. Fullback

143. Valedictory Selection

Which of the players below was *not* the first one chosen in the college draft the year he was eligible?

  a. Terry Bradshaw, quarterback, Louisiana Tech—Pittsburgh, 1970
  b. Walt Patulski, defensive end, Notre Dame—Buffalo, 1972
  c. Jim Plunkett, quarterback, Stanford—New England, 1971
  d. George Rogers, running back, South Carolina—New Orleans, 1981
  e. O.J. Simpson, running back, USC—Buffalo, 1969
  f. Randy White, defensive tackle, Maryland—Dallas, 1975

144. 100 Is Hard Enough

True or False? No NFL running back surpassed 200 yards in a single game during the 1983 regular season.

Another Papa Bear

Coach Paul (Bear) Bryant sent 10 of his college quarterbacks to the professional football ranks. From Bryant's Kentucky teams, George Blanda and Vito (Babe) Parilli went on to the NFL. While at Texas A&M, Bear coached Bobby Joe Conrad and Charley Milstead. At Alabama, his pro progeny included Joe Namath, Ken Stabler, Steve Sloan, Scott Hunter, Richard Todd, and Jeff Rutledge. On opening day of the 1977 NFL season, Namath started at quarterback for the Rams, Todd for the Jets, Hunter for the Falcons, and Stabler for the Raiders.

145. Stopped Short

Which NFL running back carried the ball 145 times for 772 yards in 1983, but did *not* score a rushing touchdown?

   a. William Andrews, Falcons
   b. Hokie Gajan, Saints
   c. Kenny King, Raiders
   d. Chuck Muncie, Chargers
   e. Tony Nathan, Dolphins
   f. Joe Washington, Redskins

146. We'll Have to See the Films

Who played Bears running back Brian Piccolo in the television movie *Brian's Song?*

   a. James Caan
   b. Robert DeNiro
   c. Peter Fonda
   d. Jack Nicholson
   e. Al Pacino
   f. Christopher Reeve

147. Great at Stopping the Dunk

Which NBA player was drafted as a defensive back by the Redskins in 1976?

   a. Quinn Buckner, Boston Celtics
   b. Adrian Dantley, Utah Jazz
   c. Magic Johnson, Los Angeles Lakers
   d. Norm Nixon, Los Angeles Clippers
   e. Sidney Mancrief, Milwaukee Bucks
   f. Kiki Vandeweghe, Portland Trailblazers

148. The Tooz Would Have Loved Him

Which lineman, listed at 7 feet, 300 pounds, played for the Raiders in 1967?

   a. Dan Birdwell
   b. Ben Davidson
   c. Ernie Ladd
   d. Carlton Oates
   e. Charles Philyaw
   f. Richard Sligh

Only a Minor Setback

Not everyone comes to the NFL through the draft. Here's a listing of some NFL players who got their starts in the minor pro leagues before making it to the NFL.

Name	Position	Minor Pro League Team
Coy Bacon	defensive end	Charleston, W.Va., Rockets
Mike Bass	safety	Detroit, Mi., Arrows
Jim Clack	center	Norfolk, Va., Neptunes
Jack Dolbin	wide receiver	Pottstown, Pa., Firebirds
Chuck Hinton	defensive tackle	Wheeling, W.Va., Ironmen
Marv Hubbard	running back	Hartford, Ct., Knights
Bob Kuechenberg	guard	Chicago, Ill., Owls
Bob Lurtsema	defensive tackle	Harrisburg, Pa. Capitols
Woody Peoples	guard	Richmond, Va., Rebels
Lou Piccone	wide receiver	Youngstown, Ohio, Hardhats
Ken Stabler	quarterback	Spokane, Wa., Shockers

149. That'll Show 'Em

Which NFC passer threw for a season-high 446 yards in one game in 1983?

a. Steve Bartkowski, Falcons
b. Dan Fouts, Chargers
c. Richard Todd, Jets
d. Joe Montana, 49ers
e. Joe Theismann, Redskins
f. Danny White, Cowboys

150. Kicking Up a Storm

True or False? Sammy Baugh is the only punter to average more than 50 yards per kick for a season.

151. From the Frying Pan into the Icebox

In 1981, the San Diego Chargers experienced a vast difference in postseason playing conditions in their AFC playoff and championship games against the Dolphins and the Bengals. Which set of figures represents the respective game-time temperatures?

    a. 99° and −59°
    b. 89° and −32°
    c. 79° and −11°
    d. 77° and 0°
    e. 68° and 3°
    f. 32° and 5°

152. It's Easier to Drive

Which NFL running back made the longest run from scrimmage in 1983?

    a. Eric Dickerson, Rams, 85 yards
    b. George Rogers, Saints, 79 yards
    c. Earl Campbell, Oilers, 78 yards
    d. Tony Dorsett, Cowboys, 75 yards
    e. Billy Sims, Lions, 73 yards
    f. Chuck Muncie, Chargers, 72 yards

Answers-NFL Trivia Quiz II

1. 1-b, 2-c, 3-d, 4-a. During the third week of the 1981 NFL season, each of the "blockers" gained more yards than the "runners" for whom they blocked in college.
2. e. Nevers scored six touchdowns and four extra points on November 28, 1929, as his Chicago Cardinals defeated the Chicago Bears 40–6.
3. 1. Ron, 2. Norm, 3. Ezra, 4. Johnnie, 5. Pete, 6. Charlie, 7. Gary, 8. Butch, 9. Cecil, 10. Ken, 11. Kenny, 12. Dan
4. c. Kupcinet played quarterback with the Philadelphia Eagles in 1935.
5. e. Ringo never played with the Steelers, but made the Pro Bowl seven times with the Packers and three times with the Eagles.
6. f. Saban played for the Cleveland Browns (1946–49), and coached the Boston Patriots (1960–61), the Buffalo Bills (1962–65, 1972–76), and the Denver Broncos (1967–1971). He was the Yankees' president 1981–83.
7. c. Jim Plunkett and Cliff Branch combined on a 99-yard touchdown reception against the Redskins on October 2, 1983.
8. a. Cannella played guard on the 1933 and 1934 Giants. He served many years as United States District Court judge for the Southern District of New York.
9. b. Dunn's grandfather was president of the University of Miami from 1926 to 1952.
10. a. Because most of his punts were "nonreturnable."
11. e. John Brodie, 49ers, and Jim Plunkett, Patriots, played quarterback. Gene Washington was converted to wide receiver with the 49ers and Dave Lewis was punting for the Bengals.
12. b. The geometric figures are called hypocyloids, but no one knows why the decals appear only on the right side of the Steelers helmet.

13. e. The New York Giants, who won the NFL championship with an 11–1–1 record, shut out 10 of 13 opponents. They lost to Cleveland 6–0 and were tied by Cleveland 0–0.

14. a. Dickinson played quarterback in 1976, the year Doug Williams was a junior at Grambling.

15. a. Huff was "miked" during a preseason game with the Bears for the program. His comments to Dewveall were most likely for the officials' benefit as much as for the education of his opponent.

16. f. White, Cowboys quarterback and son of former NFL halfback Wilford (Whizzer) White, played second base. Wills, shortstop with the Texas Rangers and son of ex-major leaguer Maury Wills, played shortstop.

17. b. Edwards, captain of the Washington Redskins, damaged his knee in 1940. Ironically, the opposing captain he met at the center of the field was Mel Hein, who also is a member of the Hall of Fame and was Edward's roommate at Washington State.

18. c. Waterfield's 20-yard pass was timed at 68.18 miles per hour.

19. e. Johnson gained 1,027 yards in 1970 and 1,182 in 1972. Price is the Giant next closest to 1,000 yards with 971 in 1951.

20. d. Until then, the Steelers had run from the single-wing formation.

21. c. Both cornerback Lane and safety Tunnell asked for tryouts, Lane with the Rams, Tunnell the Giants.

22. f. Hugh Campbell, Forrest Gregg, Les Steckel, and Sam Wyche

23. a. Lucas was chosen by the Buffalo Bills under a system by which a team took a player and then could not take another player who played that position until the team had filled all 11 offensive positions.

24. a. The Rams save a roster spot by using Corral as a kicker and punter. The Cowboys conserve a place by using White as a punter and quarterback.

25. a. Anthony Muñoz.

26. False. Joe Namath of the Jets passed for 4,007 yards in 1967. Brian Sipe of the Browns passed for 4,132 yards in 1980. Fouts also had 4,715 in 1980. Bill Kenney of the Chiefs passed for 4,348 yards in 1983, and Lynn Dickey of the Packers passed for 4,458 in 1983.

27. e. The old record was 109 set by John James of the Falcons in 1978.

28. f. White played at California.

29. 1-d, 2-c, 3-b, 4-g, 5-k, 6-e, 7-h, 8-a, 9-f, 10-i, 11-l, 12-j.

30. b. Douglass rushed for 968 yards.

31. e. Dickersen also set a new rookie rushing record with that total.

32. b. Eaton attempted two passes in 1955, his only year in the NFL, and both were incomplete. Unitas did considerably better when he earned a second chance with the Colts.

33. b. Lewis has played in 5 Super Bowls, 9 NFC championship games, 12 NFC divisional playoffs, and 1 NFC wild card game.

34. a. According to the NFL's pass rating system, Bartkowski had a 97.6 rating.

35. d

36. c. Halas represented the Decatur, Illinois, Staleys at the league's charter meeting. He was president of the Chicago Bears until his death October 31, 1984.

37. False. Campbell led all NFL rushers in each of his first three seasons, but did not do so in 1981.

38. e. Landry is no relation to Cowboys coach Tom Landry, nor did his father play in the NFL.

39. c. This distance was chosen by Camp in 1905 because it

was the maximum width the newly constructed Harvard Stadium could accommodate.

40. 1-d, 2-b, 3-h, 4-a, 5-c, 6-f, 7-l, 8-k, 9-e, 10-i, 11-g, 12-j.

41. f

42. a. Clark played for Cleveland after Brown left. Grant played for Brown at Great Lakes Naval Training Station. Michaels, Noll, and Shula played with the Browns under Brown. Walsh was a Bengals assistant.

43. d. Lane, playing offensive end, and quarterback Ogden Compton combined on the play against the Green Bay Packers on November 13, 1955.

44. f. The Seahawks made the playoffs in 1983.

45. c

46. b. Erdelatz coached the Raiders in 1960 and part of 1961.

47. d

48. c

49. a

50. f. Wilson's entire career was in the NFL with the St. Louis Cardinals, 1960–72.

51. 1-j, 2-c, 3-i, 4-h, 5-d, 6-f, 7-a, 8-b, 9-g, 10-e.

52. a

53. f. Prior to the Super Bowl, Lombardi won NFL championships in 1961, 1962, and 1965, and won Super Bowls I and II. Noll won Super Bowls IX, X, XIII, and XIV.

54. b. Meredith signed, however, with the Dallas Cowboys of the NFL.

55. a. Brown gained an NFL record of 12,312 yards in his nine-year playing career (1957–65).

56. b. Although Greene was an All-America at North Texas State, the reaction of Pittsburgh fans was less than joyous. Too many remembered such high draft picks as Mike Taylor, Don Shy, Dick Leftridge, and Bob Ferguson. More than one fan, newspaper reporter, and sports-

caster, asked, "Joe Who?" After four Super Bowls and 10 Pro Bowls, the question seldom comes up. Greene retired after the 1981 season.

57. True. John Jefferson, who had 82 catches for 1,340 yards in 1980, was traded to the Packers in 1981. Wes Chandler, his replacement, had 69 catches for 1,142 yards. Tight end Kellen Winslow had 89 for 1,290 in 1980 and a league-leading 88 for 1,075 in 1981. Wide receiver Charlie Joiner had 71 for 1,132 in 1980 and 69 for 1,142 in 1981.

58. c. Although Murray, a rookie in 1980, "shanked" the short one, he made 27 of 42 field goal attempts, including a 52-yarder on his first NFL attempt. Murray was voted to the Pro Bowl that season, and was named the game's most valuable player after kicking field goals of 31, 31, 34 and 36 yards in the NFC's 21–7 win.

59. a. Carlos Carson, Chiefs, had 1,350 to lead the AFC; Todd Christensen, Raiders, had 1,247 on 92. Prior to Kellen Winslow and Dwight Clark gaining more than 1,000 yards in receptions in 1981, the last time both AFC and NFC leading receivers gained more than 1,000 yards was in 1970 when Dick Gordon of the Bears gained 1,026 and Marlin Briscoe of the Bills gained 1,036.

60. f. Shula is in his third season as a Dolphins assistant. He is 25 years old.

61. e. Russell accomplished this against the Chargers on October 25, 1979. He had 33 attempts for the season (but not for 33 touchdowns) and gained 190 yards.

62. c. In 1981, Fouts attempted 609 passes and completed 360 for 4,802 yards. He averaged 300.1 yards per game.

63. c. Irvin, who scored on returns of 75 and 84 yards against the Falcons (October 11, 1981), broke George Atkinson's (Oakland) 1968 record of 205 yards.

64. d. Eric Dickerson, Rams, 1,808; William Andrews, Falcons, 1,567; Curt Warner, Seahawks, 1,449; Walter Payton, Bears, 1,421; John Riggins, Redskins, 1,347; Tony Dorsett, Cowboys, 1,320; Earl Campbell, Oilers, 1,301; Ottis Anderson, Cardinals, 1,270; Mike Pruitt, Browns, 1,184; George Rogers, Saints, 1,144; Joe Cribbs, Bills, 1,131; Curtis Dickey, Colts, 1,122; Tony Collins, Patriots, 1,049; Billy Sims, Lions, 1,040; Marcus Allen, Raiders, 1,014; Franco Harris, Steelers, 1,007.

65. True. Hennigan had 101 catches in 1964, Taylor 100 in 1961. Both men played in the pre-merger AFL. Johnny Morris of the Chicago Bears had 93 catches in 1964, the most receptions by an NFL/NFC receiver.

66. c. Grant was an offensive and defensive end for the Eagles in 1951 and 1952.

67. e. Henning was a quarterback with San Diego in 1966.

68. d. Harris's highest single-game total is 179 yards.

69. c. Montana completed 311 of 488 passes for a 63.7 completion percentage and 3,565 yards.

70. b. Canadeo (Packers) gained 1,052 yards in 1949. He and the others are members of the Pro Football Hall of Fame.

71. f. Walls, from Grambling, led the league with 11 interceptions. He returned them for 133 yards. Wall repeated as interception leader in 1982.

72. f. Soldier Field was opened in 1926. The Bears did not begin playing there until 1971, after it had undergone extensive renovation.

73. b. The Vikings moved into the $55 million domed facility for the 1982 season.

74. c. Fullback Gary Famiglietti and end Nick Scollard each missed on his only attempt. Scollard did make 21 of 24 extra points, though.

75. f. Dickerson's 390 carries broke George Rogers's record of 378.

76. True. Otto started 140 AFL games and went on to start 210 games over 15 seasons.
77. b. The Chicago WFL teams were the Fire (1974) and the Winds (1975). The Sting is a North American Soccer League team.
78. a. Dorsett won the trophy as a senior, Griffin won the Heisman as a junior *and* a senior—the only player ever to do so.
79. c
80. b. Campbell gained 1,450 yards in 1978 and 1,697 in 1979.
81. b. Carmichael's 61 receptions gave him a career total of 516. Charley Taylor of the Redskins (1964–77) holds the career NFL record with 649.
82. a. Although it was only for one game, the defunct Boston Yanks were the first to use Yankee Stadium in 1945. In the early days of the NFL, the 1927 New York Yankees used the stadium; the Giants became the stadium's first long-term tenant in 1956.
83. c. Griffin's touchdowns were for 38 and 52 yards.
84. True. Rashad (known then as Bobby Moore) and Cey were teammates at Mt. Tahoma High School in Tacoma, Washington, in the late 1960s.
85. e. Jim Taylor was inducted into the Hall of Fame in 1976. Atkins, Huff, Musso, and Olsen are the 1982 class of enshrinees.
86. a. 1. Rick Bryan, DT; 2 . Scott Case, S; 3. Thomas Benson, LB.
87. e. Guy was a safety and had 18 career interceptions. He is also the Raiders' "emergency" quarterback.
88. e. Hall rushed for 4,045 in his senior season, including a game in which he gained 520 yards on 11 carries. He played college football at Texas A&M.
89. b

90. e.

91. f. Olsen missed the Pro Bowl only in his final season, 1976.

92. c. Starr accomplished this during parts of the 1964 and 1965 seasons.

93. b.

94. f. The Vikings lost only three fumbles in a 16-game schedule. The Eagles lost three in 11 games in 1938.

95. c.

96. b. Hart's total of 33,858 yards ranks behind only Fran Tarkenton's 47,003 and Johnny Unitas's 40,239.

97. f. Ward and Karen Brown were married in April 1981.

98. a. Anderson received his law degree in 1981 from Chase Law School at Northern Kentucky University.

99. f. Wright's totals were three receptions for 62 yards and three touchdowns.

100. False. Jan Stenerud (Chiefs) won the award for kicking four field goals (23, 25, 42, and 48 yards) and two extra points in 1972. Garo Yepremian (Dolphins) accounted for all AFC points in 1974 with five field goals (16, 27, 37, 41, and 42 yards) in a 15–13 victory. Murray won his award in 1981. Nick Lowery of the Chiefs was a co-winner with Lee Roy Selmon, defensive end of the Buccaneers, in 1982 for kicking a 23-yard field goal with three seconds to play.

101. c. The closest the Saints have come are an 8–8–0 records in 1979 and 1983.

102. b. Lou Groza (1946–59, 1961–67), Sam Baker (1960), and Don Cockroft (1968–80).

103. True. The Lions have had Howard (Hopalong) Cassady (1955), Leon Hart (1949), Steve Owens (1969), Billy Sims (1978), Frank Sinkwich (1942), and Doak Walker (1948). The Rams have had Terry Baker (1962), John Cappelletti (1973), Glenn Davis (1946), Les Horvath (1944), Tom Harmon (1940), and Bruce Smith (1941).

104. b. Campbell rushed for 1,934 yards in 1980—second only to Simpson's 1973 record total of 2,003.

105. e.

106. True. Fears caught 18 passes against the Packers on December 3, 1950. Joe Carter of the Eagles and Morris (Red) Badgro of the Giants shared the league lead for 1934 with 16 receptions each.

107. c. Nevers, who played baseball in 1927 and 1928 with the St. Louis Browns of the American League, gave up Ruth's eighth and forty-first home runs.

108. c. Ilkin's family emigrated to the United States when he was two and settled in the Chicago area. Ilkin attended Indiana State.

109. b. Hardy threw eight interceptions to the Philadelphia Eagles on September 24, 1950. All others listed suffered seven interceptions in one game.

110. f. Before Tubbs took over the position in 1960, Patera played middle linebacker. Tubbs held the position 1960–65, Jordan 1966–76, and Breunig from 1977 to date.

111. f. Glazebrook was cut three times before finally making the team. He acquired the nickname because TWX is the teletype system used by NFL teams to report waiver moves to the league office.

112. e. Stenerud kicked record 48-yard field goals in Super Bowl IV and the 1972 Pro Bowl. Stenerud was a member of the Chiefs at the time. He now plays for the Packers.

113. b. Not only did the Giants use a boat to make the trip to Providence, but they took the fabled Staten Island Ferry several times when they played the Stapleton Stapes on Stapleton's home field.

114. c. Haynes, from North Texas State, led the AFL in rushing with 875 yards.

115. e. Torgeson was in Pittsburgh with linebacker Bill (1964–68), in Washington with guard Ron (1976–77 and 1981), and in Los Angeles with center Rich (1978–80).

116. d. On November 6, 1934, the Philadelphia Eagles defeated the Cincinnati Reds (not the baseball team) 64–0.

117. c. Nelson had his 101-yard return against Dallas, September 26, 1971, and his 100-yard return against Cleveland, December 11, 1966. Both were for touchdowns.

118. b. Benton compiled 303 yards on 10 receptions against the Lions on November 22, 1945. At the time the Rams were located in Cleveland.

119. f. Winslow had five scoring receptions against Oakland on November 22, 1981.

120. a. Agajanian's career spanned 19 years, 1946–64. His NFL teams are the Steelers and Eagles, 1945; Giants, 1949 and 1954–57; Rams 1953, and Packers, 1961. In the AAFC he played with the Los Angeles Dons 1947–48. He played in the AFL with the Los Angeles Chargers 1960; Dallas Texans 1961; Oakland Raiders 1962; and the San Diego Chargers, 1964.

121. a. The Colts sacked Cardinals passers 12 times on October 26, 1980. The Steelers recorded their sacks against the Cowboys on November 20, 1966.

122. c. Foreman led the NFC in scoring with 132 points, in receiving with 73 receptions, but trailed Jim Otis in rushing, 1,070 yards to 1,076.

123. b. Because yards lost attempting to pass (sacks) are subtracted from a team's net passing yardage, the Packers had–10 and the Cowboys–1.

124. a. The Colts, along with the Browns and Steelers, joined the 10 American Football League teams to form the AFC in the 1970 realignment.

125. b. Humm and Stabler played for Oakland from 1975 to 1979.

126. e. Regular-season teammates. Pastorini and Burrough combined on a 64-yard touchdown in the 1976 game.

127. True. That team, which won Super Bowl XIV, was composed entirely of draft choices (39) or free agents (6) signed originally by the Steelers.

128. b. Ron gained 1,027 yards in 1970 and 1,182 in 1972 for the New York Giants. Alex led the American League with a .329 average in 1970 for the California Angels.

129. d. Karras finished second to fullback John David Crow of Texas A&M. Karras, an All-America, played with the Detroit Lions from 1958 to 1970.

130. e. Before joining the Chargers in 1963, Roy had many years experience operating a health studio in Baton Rouge, Louisiana, where one of his students was 1959 Heisman Trophy winner Billy Cannon of Louisiana State. Cannon played with the Oilers, Raiders, and Chiefs, 1960–70.

131. e. The towns of Mauch Chunk and East Mauch Chunk, Pennsylvania, became known as Jim Thorpe in 1954. Jim Thorpe is buried there.

132. c. Hinkle led the league most of the 1943 season. However, the "Steagles" finished their schedule on December 5, and Paschal's team, the Giants, still had a game to play on December 12. Paschal, who went into the game in fourth place, gained 92 yards and ended the season with 572 yards to Hinkle's 571.

133. True. Fouts completed 33 of 53 attempts for 433 yards, and Strock completed 29 of 42 for 403 yards.

134. f. Pepitone, who played first base for the Yankees of the American League (1962–69), was the original Broadway Joe. Namath was given the nickname in 1965 when he joined the Jets.

135. c. Halas coached the Bears for 40 seasons (1920–29, 1933–42, 1946–55, and 1958–67). Lambeau coached the Packers 29 years (1921–49).

136. b. Hornung scored 176 points in 1960 on 15 touchdowns, 41 extra points, and 15 field goals. The next highest total is 155 points scored by Gino Cappelletti of the Boston Patriots in 1964 on 7 touchdowns, 38 extra points, and 25 field goals. Note: For record purposes the NFL recognizes AFL totals.

137. d. The Spalding J5 was the official intercollegiate football of that era, which also was used in the NFL.

138. b. Berry had 12 receptions in the 1958 NFL Championship Game, which, like the Dolphins-Chargers game, also was a sudden-death overtime game. John Stallworth of Pittsburgh had 10 receptions in the 1978 divisional playoff game against Denver.

139. f. The Portsmouth Spartans were in the NFL from 1930 to 1933. Detroit interests bought the team and moved the franchise in 1934.

140. f. Lowe averaged 4.87 yards-per-carry (4,995 yards on 1,026 attempts) with the Chargers (1960–68) and the Chiefs (1968–69).

141. f.

142. b. The term ''tight end'' did not come into use until the 1960s, when Ron Kramer of the Packers, Mike Ditka of the Bears, and John Mackey of the Colts combined receiving with blocking ability.

143. f. White was the Cowboy's first choice, but the second player overall. Steve Bartkowski (quarterback, California) was taken by the Falcons and was the first 1975 draft choice.

144. False. James Wilder of the Buccaneers led NFC rushers with 219 yards against the Vikings; Tony Collins of the Patriots led AFC runners with 212 against the Jets.

145. c.

146. a. Caan played Piccolo, who died of cancer, in the 1970 movie.

147. a. Buckner played football at Indiana early in his col-

lege career, before concentrating on basketball. He never
played with the Redskins.

148. f. Sligh, who played defensive tackle only that one
season, is the biggest man to play pro football. He was
from North Carolina College.

149. c. Todd was traded to the Saints for the 1984 season.

150. True. Baugh averaged 51.4 for the Redskins in 1940.
Yale Lary of the Lions has the next-highest average,
48.9 in 1963.

151. c. Taking the wind chill factor (−59°) in Cincinnati into
account, the Chargers experienced a temperature change
of 128°. The humidity in Miami was above 90 percent.

152. a.

NFL Photo Trivia

Pictures worth 1,000 yards

1. Extraterrestrial End

In the picture above, former split end Raymond Berry of the Baltimore Colts is:

a. Working as Lloyd Bridges's stand-in during a *Sea Hunt* episode dealing with pro football.

b. Wearing goggles he devised to combat the late-winter sun in Los Angeles during a Colts-Rams game.

c. Wearing goggles he uses as a wlder in the offseason.

d. Wearing goggles he devised when his contact lenses were damaged earlier in the season.

e. All of the above.

f. None of the above.

2. Wersching Machine

In Super Bowl XVI, 49ers kicker Ray Wersching was responsible for the two fastest scores in Super Bowl competition to that time. How much time elapsed between his field goals?

    a. 13 seconds
    b. 20 seconds
    c. 27 seconds
    d. 36 seconds
    e. 48 seconds
    f. 59 seconds

3. Hewitt's Law

Bill Hewitt (pictured above, center) played end several years
for the Chicago Bears and the Philadelphia Eagles without a
helmet. A number of other NFL players of the era also
refused to wear headgear. After a three-year retirement, Hewitt
came back for one more season only to find a helmet was
required. In what year did the NFL make wearing a helmet
mandatory?

   a. 1929
   b. 1933
   c. 1937
   d. 1940
   e. 1943
   f. 1949

4. Habitual Defender

Safety Ken Houston (29) of the Oilers is about to score a touchdown on the return of an intercepted pass to establish an all-time career record. Of his 49 lifetime interceptions, how many did he return for touchdowns?

    a. 7
    b. 9
    c. 12
    d. 14
    e. 17
    f. 21

5. Money Talks

William (Pudge) Heffelfinger, Yale's immortal All-America guard, is known as the first pro football player. What was the one-time salary paid to him by the Allegheny Athletic Association of Pittsburgh for its game against the Pittsburgh Athletic Club on November 12, 1892?

  a. $10
  b. ''$10 and cakes''
  c. $50
  d. $100
  e. $500
  f. $1,000

6. How Pedestrian

Who is the man in street clothes who appears to be leading interference for Eagles running back Timmy Brown (22)?

  a. A fan
  b. Cardinals head coach Charley Winner
  c. Eagles offensive coordinator Jerry Williams
  d. Cardinals defensive coordinator Chuck Drulis
  e. A free agent looking for a pro tryout
  f. None of the above

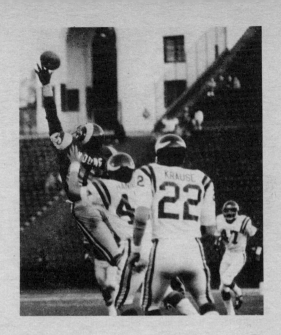

7. Deflected Glory

This 1979 photo shows:

- a. The last Rams game played in Los Angeles's Memorial Coliseum.
- b. Rams tight end Charle Young (86) about to make a game-winning, one-handed catch after the ball was first touched by a Rams teammate.
- c. Vikings safety Paul Krause (22) about to make an interception of the pass deflected by Young, which will set the all-time NFL career record for interceptions.
- d. Young about to tip the ball to guard Dennis Harrah (not shown) for a 67-yard touchdown; the longest ever by an interior offensive lineman.
- e. The last play of the NFL's longest game.
- f. Young's catch to set a receiving record for NFL tight ends.

8. Famous Faces

The three men pictured are:

a. All members of the Pro Football Hall of Fame.
b. All immortalized on Mt. Rushmore.
c. All football players who became United States Presidents.
d. A member of the Pro Football Hall of Fame and two United States Presidents he played against.
e. Future Commissioners of the NFL.
f. United States Senators from Ohio.

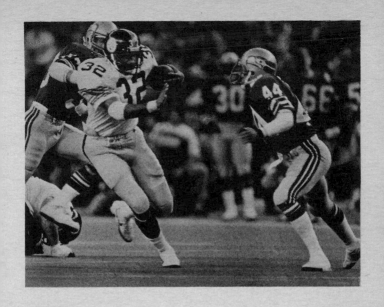

9. Milestone

On this play against the Seahawks on November 8, 1981, Franco Harris became:

    a. The all-time leading NFL career rushing record-holder.
    b. The first running back to surpass 1,000 yards that early in a season.
    c. The third man in NFL history to rush for more than 10,000 career yards.
    d. The NFL career leader in rushing touchdowns.
    e. All of the above.
    f. None of the above.

10. NFL Roots

Pictured above are:

   a. Jim Thorpe and his Carlisle teammates at their 15-year class reunion.

   b. A barnstorming team sponsored by Buffalo Bill's Wild West Show and Congress of Rough Riders of the World.

   c. The Yale intramural champions of 1921.

   d. The 1922 Oorang Indians.

   e. The 1926 Duluth Eskimos.

   f. The Hominy, Oklahoma, Indians team that beat the New York Giants in an exhibition game.

11. Don't Damage the Profile

Who is the former NFL halfback and Pro Football Hall of Fame member about to take a hard right from Tony Curtis in the 1953 feature film *All-American?*

    a. Raymond Berry, Colts
    b. Frank Gifford, Giants
    c. Hugh McElhenny, 49ers
    d. Pat Summerall, Giants
    e. Charley Trippi, Chicago Cardinals
    f. Bill Wade, Rams

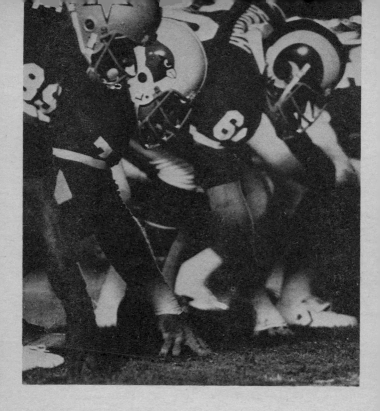

12. Men of Many Hats

Why are the three linemen shown wearing helmets from three different teams?

   a. The helmets are being worn by semipro players during a preseason tryout.

   b. They are the only helmets which fit the players.

   c. They are part of the cast of the 1962 science fiction movie *Run to Jupiter*.

   d. They are participants in the AFC-NFC Pro Bowl.

   e. They are members of a wartime merger team in a 1943 game against the "Steagles."

   f. They are playing in an NFL old-timers game.

13. Pioneer Coach

Pictured above is the first black to be a head coach in the NFL. Who is he?

  a. Joe Lillard, Chicago Cardinals, 1932
  b. Bobby (Rube) Marshall, Rock Island, Illinois, Independents, 1921
  c. Fritz Pollard, Akron, Ohio, Pros, 1920
  d. Paul Robeson, Milwaukee, Wisconsin, Badgers, 1922
  e. Fred (Duke) Slater, Chicago Cardinals, 1926
  f. Jay (Inky) Williams, Dayton, Ohio, Triangles, 1924

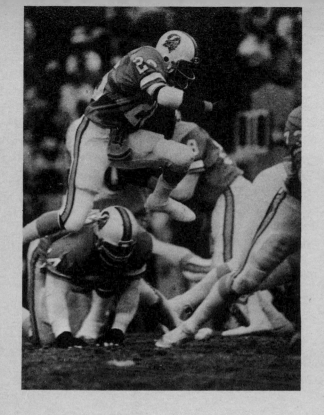

14. Before and After

Who is the player pictured above (26) and what did he accomplish before coming to the NFL?

- a. Archie Griffin, who won the Heisman Trophy twice.
- b. George Rogers, who was the first player taken in the 1981 NFL draft.
- c. James Owens, a former Olympic hurdler.
- d. Tony Dorsett, who set the NCAA record for career rushing yardage.
- e. Wade Manning, who was a baseball player in college.
- f. Johnny Dirden, who drove a cement truck before his free agent tryout.

15. Cast in Bronze

Dick McCann, the man pictured above, was:

a. The former NFL player who supervised the carving of Mt. Rushmore.
b. The former NFL executive who became a noted sculptor.
c. The publicist who gave Notre Dame's Four Horsemen their nickname.
d. The first general manager of the Washington Redskins.
e. The first commissioner of the AFL.
f. None of the above.

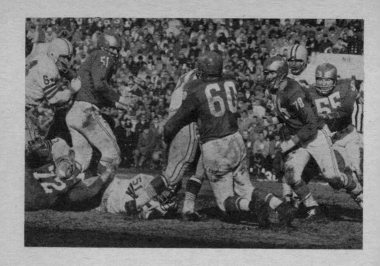

16. Once Is Enough

This photograph from the 1960 NFL championship game shows Chuck Bednarik (60) of the Eagles tackling Jim Taylor (31) of the Packers. The photo is significant because:

   a. It was the last time the Eagles were world champions.
   b. The game was the only championship game the Packers ever lost under Vince Lombardi.
   c. It shows the last time a player (Bednarik) played offense and defense extensively in a championship game.
   d. It shows the final play of the game.
   e. All of the above.
   f. None of the above.

17. Turning on the Juice

What is O.J. Simpson (above, center) doing?

    a. Announcing his retirement from the NFL.
    b. Chairing a board meeting of the Buffalo Electric Power Company.
    c. Holding a press conference after setting the all-time NFL single-season rushing record.
    d. Acting in the final scene of the feature film *Run, Juice, Run*.
    e. Reacting to his trade to the 49ers.
    f. Accepting the Heisman Trophy.

18. Quantity for Quality

Why are Ollie Matson and Les Richter surrounded by 20 helmets in this 1959 photograph?

a. They are the last active members of the Rams' 1951 championship team.

b. Matson and Richter ran against each other for a United States Congressional seat.

c. The helmets represent the number of players traded by the Rams to obtain Matson and Richter.

d. They are participating in a training camp drill called "bull in the ring."

e. They each scored 10 touchdowns that season.

f. They were co-captains of the Rams' 1958 championship team.

19. Opening the Flood Gates

This photo shows the opening play from scrimmage in the 1940 championship game between the Chicago Bears and the Washington Redskins. Who won and by what score?

a. Washington, 62–14
b. Chicago, 56–0
c. Washington, 48–3
d. Chicago, 69–6
e. Washington, 56–0
f. Chicago, 73–0

20. History of Pro Football, 101

This photograph of the 1902 Shelby, Ohio, Athletic Club Blues is significant because:

a. They were the first team to use shin guards.
b. The black player (extreme right, second row) later became the first black pro football player.
c. Baseball executive Branch Rickey (extreme right, standing) owned the team.
d. Reginald Fauntleroy (middle, front row) became the youngest person ever to play pro football.
e. The team played all its home games indoors at the Shelby National Guard Armory.
f. None of the above.

21. Finally Benched

The Lions ball carrier in this 1940 photograph:

a. Played running back longer than anyone else in the NFL, 19 seasons.

b. Was the first to use heavy weights in an offseason training program.

c. Later became a United States Supreme Court justice.

d. Led the NFL in rushing each year he played.

e. Signed the highest-paying contract in NFL history.

f. All of the above.

22. Into Orbit

Pictured above is Tom Dempsey of the Saints kicking the NFL's longest field goal on November 8, 1970. How long was the kick?

  a. 50 yards
  b. 56 yards
  c. 57 yards
  d. 59 yards
  e. 63 yards
  f. 74 yards

23. Law of Averages

Jeris White (with the ball) and his Tampa Bay teammates are celebrating a 33–14 victory over the Saints on December 11, 1977. What was the two-year-old Buccaneers' overall record going into that game?

    a. 0–0–26
    b. 22–2–2
    c. 0–20–6
    d. 12–14–0
    e. 26–0–0
    f. 0–26–0

24. The Sting

A close look at the photo above will show the head coach (extreme right), an assistant coach (left, in street clothes), and several players signaling to the player (70) with the ball. What are they trying to tell him?

a. He has a first down.
b. Get out of bounds and stop the clock.
c. His interception has made them number-one in their division.
d. He's running the wrong way.
e. There's still time for one more play.
f. His wife just had a baby boy.

25. No Lack of Depth

Before the NFL was organized in 1920, the Columbus, Ohio, Panhandles were one of the most powerful pro teams. Who are the six men pictured above?

    a. Head coach Glenn (Pop) Warner (far left) and his staff.
    b. Knute Rockne and five Notre Dame players.
    c. The six Nesser brothers.
    d. The four Nesser brothers and the two Smith brothers.
    e. The team's starting backfield and ends.
    f. Six former Ohio State players who went on to play with the Panhandles.

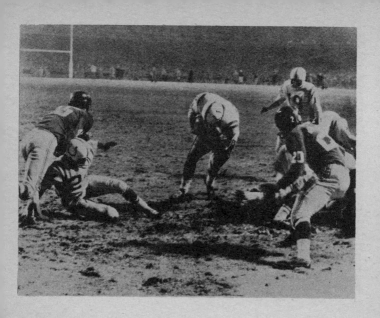

26. Did They Get Time-and-a-Half?

In the photo above, Alan (The Horse) Ameche of the Colts is scoring the winning touchdown in the 1958 NFL championship game against the New York Giants. What made the game so significant?

   a. It was Baltimore's third straight NFL championship.
   b. It was the first "sudden death overtime" championship game.
   c. It marked Johnny Unitas's NFL debut.
   d. Ameche scored six touchdowns, an NFL record.
   e. The game went into two overtime periods.
   f. Baltimore held New York scoreless.

27. Someone to Look Up to

True or False? At 5 feet 4 inches, Atlanta kick returner Reggie Smith (pictured above) is the shortest man ever to play in the NFL.

28. Made in Hollywood

This 1949 movie poster shows several of the NFL's premier quarterbacks in Rams helmets: Sammy Baugh of the Redskins, Frank (Boley) Dancewicz of the Boston Yanks, Indian Jack Jacobs of the Packers, and Sid Luckman of the Bears. Besides its cast, what was the film's significance?

   a. It was the first time players from each league city appeared in the same film.
   b. It was the first film use of NFL helmet logos.
   c. Six of the players pictured in the movie poster are in the Pro Football Hall of Fame.
   d. Most players in the film wore Rams helmets to take advantage of existing game film.
   e. All of the above.
   f. None of the above.

29. Can I have the Car Keys, Coach?

Shown above in 1981 are Colts wide receiver David Shula (in football pants) and Dolphins head coach Don Shula. This father-son combination was unique because:

    a. Don Shula was the first NFL head coach with a son playing in the league.
    b. Player-son David replaced his father as Miami's head coach.
    c. David played in the league for a head coach other than his father.
    d. Don Shula traded his son to another team.
    e. David was the fourth son of an NFL head coach to play in the NFL.
    f. David was the only son of an NFL head coach who was not a quarterback.

30. "Outlined Against the Gray October Sky . . ."

True or False? The famous Four Horsemen backfield of Notre Dame's 1924 team never played pro football.

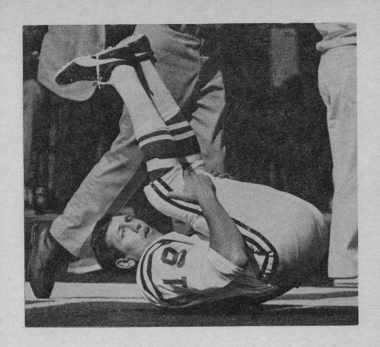

31. The Age of Aquarius

What are two things that make the above photograph of Pro Football Hall of Fame quarterback Johnny Unitas unique?

a. He is wearing low-cut shoes and long hair.
b. He is wearing jersey number 19 (instead of 12) and he never did pregame warmups.
c. He is in a Baltimore uniform and never before wore white socks.
d. He is wearing a mesh jersey for the first time and played the entire game without a helmet.
e. His helmet came off when he was sacked, the only sack of his career.
f. He pulled a hamstring during pregame warmups and missed playing his second Super Bowl game.

32. Les Is More

Pictured above is Les Bingaman (65) of the Lions. What made Bingaman so notable?

  a. He led the league in tackles three seasons in a row.
  b. He put on a one-man goal-line stand against the Bears in the 1952 NFL Championship Game.
  c. He ran the NFL's first electronically timed 4.3-second 40-yard dash.
  d. He was the heaviest man to play in the NFL.
  e. He was the last man to play without a facemask.
  f. He originated the 3-4 defense.

33. A Dynamic Duo of One

On December 8, 1957, rookie halfback Eddie Sutton of the Redskins scored on a 17-yard pass play. Later, playing defensive back, he intercepted a pass. Name the most recent player to score on a pass reception and make an interception in the same game.

    a. Jim Dooley, Bears
    b. Roy Green, Cardinals
    c. John Jefferson, Packers
    d. James Lofton, Packers
    e. Dave Logan, Browns
    f. Emlen Tunnell, Giants

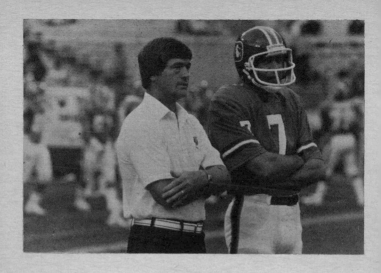

34. Familiarity Breeds Respect

Shown above in this 1981 photograph were first-year head coach Dan Reeves of the Broncos and his quarterback, Craig Morton (7). What is significant about the pair?

    a. Both were college quarterbacks.
    b. Both were rookie quarterbacks with the Cowboys in 1965.
    c. Morton is a year older than his coach.
    d. Reeves was Morton's coach at Dallas (1970–72).
    e. All of the above.
    f. None of the above.

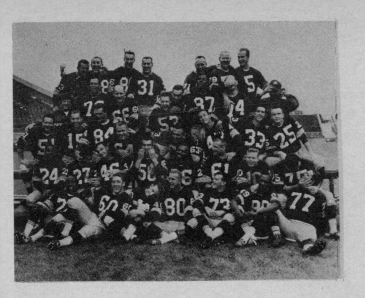

35. A Moment of Levity

The 1962 Green Bay Packers are:

   a. On a team trip to Disneyland.
   b. Celebrating the 1962 NFL championship, their third in a row.
   c. Laughing at Vince Lombardi's latest joke.
   d. Just goofing off.
   e. Celebrating the opening of training camp.
   f. Getting ready to break the telephone-booth-stuffing record.

36. It's All in the Wrist

What was Tom Matte wearing on his wrist and why?
  a. A wristband to support a sprain.
  b. A wrist microphone to communicate with the coaches in the press box.
  c. A digital watch to keep the offical game time.
  d. A pulse monitor, part of an NFL medical study.
  e. A wristband with the Colts' game plan written on it.
  f. A pouch containing a good-luck piece.

Answers-NFL Photo Trivia

1. b. Berry, a member of the Pro Football Hall of Fame, first used these "sunglasses"—modified from underwater goggles—in 1958.

2. a.

3. e. Hewitt, a member of the Pro Football Hall of Fame, played 1932–36 with the Bears, 1937–39 with the Eagles, and came back for a final season with the 1943 Philadelphia/Pittsburgh "Steagles."

4. b. Ironically, Houston's record-setting interception came one play after he had returned an eighth interception for a score. Both passes were thrown by John Hadl (number 21 in the photo) of the Chargers on December 19, 1971.

5. e. Heffelfinger denied ever playing pro football, but a ledger sheet from the Allegheny Athletic Association is on display at the Pro Football Hall of Fame in Canton, Ohio, with an entry "W. Heffelfinger for playing—cash—$500.00." Until this was revealed, it was thought that John Brallier, who received $10 and cakes from the Latrobe, Pennsylvania, team in 1895, was the first player to receive payment for playing.

6. b. Winner was very close to the sideline on this play. To avoid a collision he moved onto the playing field instead of moving backward.

7. c. Krause's interception was number 80 in his career, which broke Emlen Tunnell's record. Krause made another interception in this game, and retired at the end of the season.

8. d. Pictured, left to right are George Musso, Ronald Reagan, and Gerald Ford. While at Millikin, Musso, a former guard and tackle with the Chicago Bears who was elected to the Pro Football Hall of Fame in 1982, played against Reagan, who was a guard for Eureka College. As a member of the 1935 Bears, Musso played against Ford, a center from Michigan who played on the college All-Star team that year.

9. c. Harris needs 363 yards in 1984 to become the NFL's all-time rusher.

10. d. The Team was based in Marion, Ohio, and was sponsored by the noted Oorang Airedale Kennels of nearby LaRue. Jim Thorpe (top row, center) was the coach of the team that included native Americans Arrowhead, Big Bear, Black Bear, Pete Calac, Deadeye, Eagle Feather, Gray Horse, Joe Guyon, Joe Little Twig, Lone Wolf, Bemus Pierce, Red Fang, Red Foot, Red Fox, Running Deer, Tom St. Germaine, Baptiste Thunder, and Wrinkle Meat.

11. b. Gifford, like many USC football players of his era, was cast as an extra in several films. In his early years with the Giants, he continued to appear in movies during the offseason.

12. d. The photograph was taken at the 1979 Pro Bowl, which was the first time (since the game was reinstituted in 1951) that players wore the helmets of their respective teams. Shown are tight end Billy Joe DuPree of the Cowboys, tackle Dan Dierdorf of the Cardinals, and guard Dennis Harrah of the Rams.

13. c. Pollard served as head coach at Akron in 1920, the first year of the NFL. He later coached at Hammond, Indiana, in 1923 and 1925 when that team was a member of the league.

14. c. Owens placed sixth in the high hurdles in the 1976 Summer Olympics at Montreal.

15. f. McCann served 16 years as the Redskins' general manager (1947–62), then became the first director of the Pro Football Hall of Fame (1962–67).

16. e. After taking a 17–13 lead late in the game, the Eagles were attempting to stop the Packers. Quarterback Bart Starr was driving the team deep into Eagles territory as time was running out. Taylor took a swing pass and broke several tackles before Bednarik wrapped him up at the 9. Bednarik stayed on top of Taylor as the final seconds elapsed, assuring the Eagles' victory.

17. c. Simpson is holding a locker-room press conference

after surpassing 2,000 yards (2,003) in the final game of 1973. Meeting the press with him are the players who blocked for him during the season.

18. c. Richter, a linebacker, was traded by the Dallas Texans in 1952 for 11 players: quarterback David Anderson, halfback Billy Baggett, tackle Jack Halliday, fullback Dick Hoerner, defensive back Tom Keane, fullback Dick McKissack, center Aubrey (Red) Phillips, center Joe Reid, halfback George Sims, guard Vic Vasicek, and end Dick Wilkins.

Matson, a running back, was traded by the Chicago Cardinals in 1959 for nine players: halfback Don Brown, defensive tackle Frank Fuller, defensive tackle Art Hauser, fullback Larry Hickman, defensive end Glenn Holtzmann, tackle Ken Panfil, and end John Tracey. The Rams also gave up their second-and fourth-round 1960 draft choices, which the Cardinals used to select guard Mike McGee of Duke and end Silas Woods of Marquette.

19. f. Bill Osmanski, shown carrying the ball in the photo, ran 68 yards for a touchdown on the first play from scrimmage. It was all downhill from there for the Redskins.

20. b. The black man is halfback Charley Follis, who became the first black pro when he signed a contract in 1904 with the Blues, which were then a pro team.

21. c. The player with the ball is Byron R. (Whizzer) White, who played with the Pittsburgh Pirates (now the Steelers) in 1938 and the Lions in 1940 and 1941. He led the league in rushing in 1938 and 1940. White was appointed to the Supreme Court by President John F. Kennedy in 1962.

22. e. Dempsey's kick came on the final play of the game, and provided the winning margin in a 19–17 victory over the Lions.

23. f. The Buccaneers had not won a game during their first season (1976), and had lost their first 12 games of 1977

before defeating the Saints 33–14. Tampa Bay had six interceptions in the game (one by White) and ran three back for touchdowns.

24. d. On October 28, 1964, Vikings defensive end Jim Marshall picked up a fumble at the 40 yard line and headed toward the end zone. He thought he scored a 60-yard touchdown for the Vikings, but actually scored a safety (two points) for the 49ers. Nevertheless, the Vikings won 27–22.

25. c. The six Nessers played several years together during the World War I era. Pictured left to right are: Ted, John, Phil, Al, Frank, and Fred.

26. b. Ameche scored on a one-yard off-tackle slant with 8:15 elapsed in overtime. The game, one of the first witnessed by millions of television viewers nationwide, is still considered by many "the greatest game ever played." It did much to popularize the game of pro football.

27. False. Smith, a half-inch shorter than the late Buddy Young (former Colts halfback and present-day NFL league office executive) was believed to be the all-time shortest. But after learning about Smith, Jack Shapiro, a halfback on the 1929 Staten Island Stapletons, came forth with documentation to the contrary. Shapiro produced his World War II discharge papers, which listed his height at 5 feet ½ inch.

28. e. *Triple Threat* starred a player from each 1948 NFL team and was made in cooperation with the NFL during the last year of the intense rivalry with the All-America Football Conference. Many players wore Rams helmets so actual Rams game films could be used for the action sequences. Baugh, Dudley, Luckman, Trippi, Van Buren, and Waterfield are in the Hall of Fame.

29. c. The Third son of an NFL head coach to play in the league, David is a wide receiver with the Colts. The two other sons of NFL head coaches are George Wilson, Jr., who played quarterback at Miami in 1966 while his

father was head coach, and John McKay, Jr., who played wide receiver at Tampa Bay (1976–78) while his father was head coach.

30. False. Harry Stuhldreher, quarterback, played for the Brooklyn Lions and the Brooklyn Horsemen (AFL) in 1926; Elmer Layden, fullback, played for the Brooklyn Horsemen (AFL) in 1926; Jim Crowley, left halfback, played for the Green Bay Packers and the Providence, Rhode Island, Steamroller in 1925; and Don Miller, right halfback, also played for Providence in 1925.

31. a. Unitas's flat-top crewcut and hightop black shoes were as much his trademarks as jersey number 19 and touchdown passes. He is pictured above warming up for the only game of his 18-year career in which he wore lowcut shoes. It was also the first season, 1970, he wore "long" hair. The photo was taken prior to kickoff Super Bowl V, January 17, 1971. All players wore recently developed turf shoes because of the Orange Bowl's artificial playing surface.

32. d. Bingaman, who played middle guard from 1948 to 1954, could not be weighed on a locker room scale. At training camp in 1954, he was taken to a local feed and grain mill in Ypsilanti, Michigan, where the Lions trained, and registered 349½ pounds on a feed scale.

33. b. Green, normally a safety and a kick returner, scored on a 58-yard touchdown pass while playing wide receiver. That same day (September 20, 1981), he made an interception. Sutton, who is now a physician in Fresno, California, says, "I figure I'm still one up on Green, although he's a fantastic athlete. I completed a halfback option pass [to Leo Elter for 21 yards] that day." Green continued to start at wide receiver *and* play safety throughout the 1981 season. Presently he's strictly a wide receiver.

One week after Green's feat, Cleveland wide receiver Dave Logan, used as a defensive back late in a game against Atlanta, intercepted a pass. He already had made two receptions on offense (neither for a score).

34. e

35. d. Although this photo never had wide circulation, it seemed a paradox that Lombardi, known for his discipline, would allow such frivolity. Lombardi was not present at the time the photo was taken and became quite angry over the team's "unprofessional" attitude when he later saw it.

36. e. Late in the 1965 season, Colts running back Matte, a former quarterback at Ohio State, was forced to play in place of injured Baltimore quarterbacks Johnny Unitas and Gary Cuozzo. In the Divisional Playoff Game December 26 against the Packers, Matte wore a wrist band with the Colts' key offensive plays written on it. The Packers won the sudden-death overtime game 13–10; the wristband went to the Pro Football Hall of Fame.

Super Trivia

More than fifty questions about the first XIX Super Bowls

1. Northern Lights

Which northern city has hosted the Super Bowl?

a. Buffalo
b. Chicago
c. Minneapolis
d. New York
e. Pontiac
f. Seattle

2. One Step Up

Which Super Bowl most valuable player later became head coach of the team for which he played?

a. Terry Bradshaw
b. Len Dawson
c. Chuck Howley
d. Joe Namath
e. Jake Scott
f. Bart Starr

3. Seeing Both Sides

Who is the only player to start one Super Bowl on defense and another on offense?

a. Terry Bradshaw
b. Mike Curtis
c. E.J. Holub
d. Max McGee
e. Mel Renfro
f. None of the above

4. Creating a Tough Encore

Which coach won the Super Bowl in his first season as head coach?

    a. Tom Flores, Oakland Raiders
    b. Joe Gibbs, Redskins
    c. Don McCafferty, Baltimore Colts
    d. Red Miller, Denver Broncos
    e. Chuck Noll, Pittsburgh Steelers
    f. Don Shula, Miami Dolphins

5. Early Dominance

True or False? Of the four Super Bowls played between the AFL and the NFL prior to realignment in 1970, the NFL won three.

6. Six-Pack

True or False? Six members of the Green Bay Packers' starting lineup in Super Bowl I eventually were enshrined in the Pro Football Hall of Fame.

7. Opening Act

Which quarterback started the 1980 regular season opener for the Super Bowl XV champion Oakland Raiders?

    a. George Blanda
    b. Tom Flores
    c. Ron Jaworski
    d. Dan Pastorini
    e. Jim Plunkett
    f. Marc Wilson

8. Triple Theft

Who holds the record with three interceptions in a Super Bowl game?

    a. Randy Beverly, New York Jets
    b. Mel Blount, Pittsburgh
    c. Chuck Howley, Dallas
    d. Rod Martin, Oakland
    e. Jake Scott, Miami
    f. All of the above

9. Long Distance Operator

Which player holds the Super Bowl record for the longest run from scrimmage?

    a. Lance ALworth, Dallas
    b. Larry Csonka, Miami
    c. Kenny King, Oakland
    d. Franco Harris, Pittsburgh
    e. Marcus Allen, Los Angeles Raiders
    f. Wendell Tyler, Los Angeles Rams

10. Coast-to-Coast

Which player holds the Super Bowl record for the longest pass reception?

    a. Willie Brown, Oakland
    b. Kenny King, Oakland
    c. John Mackey, Baltimore
    d. Ahmad Rashad, Minnesota
    e. John Stallworth, Pittsburgh
    f. Howard Twilley, Miami

11. Lucky Eleven

Which player holds the Super Bowl record for the most receptions (11) in one game?

    a. Lance Alworth, Dallas
    b. John Henderson, Minnesota
    c. Dan Ross, Cincinnati
    d. George Sauer, New York Jets
    e. John Stallworth, Pittsburgh
    f. Lynn Swann, Pittsburgh

12. Double Your Pleasure

Which of the players below scored two rushing touchdowns in one Super Bowl game?

    a. Pete Banaszak, Oakland, Super Bowl XI
    b. Larry Csonka, Miami, Super Bowl VIII
    c. Franco Harris, Pittsburgh, Super Bowl XIV
    d. Elijah Pitts, Green Bay, Super Bowl I
    e. Marcus Allen, Los Angeles Raiders, Super Bowl XVIII
    f. All of the above

13. Kicking Up a Storm

Which two players each kicked five extra points in one Super Bowl game?

    a. George Blanda, Raiders; Effren Herrera, Cowboys; and Max McGee, Packers
    b. Don Chandler, Packers; Roy Gerela, Steelers; and Chris Bahr, Raiders
    c. Russell Erxleben, Saints; Effren Herrera, Cowboys; and Jim Turner, Jets

d. Mike Clark, Cowboys; Jan Stenerud, Chiefs, and Jan Stenerud, Packers

e. Matt Bahr, Steelers; Jim Turner, Broncos; and Mark Moseley, Redskins

f. Garo Yepremian, Dolphins; Mike Bragg, Redskins; and Mike Mercer, Raiders

14. Hot Streak

Which player completed six of the seven passes he attempted in a Super Bowl game?

a. Terry Bradshaw, Steelers
b. Len Dawson, Chiefs
c. Bob Griese, Dolphins
d. Robert Newhouse, Cowboys
e. Jim Plunkett, Raiders
f. Joe Montana, 49ers

15. Innocent Bystander

Which player wore two Super Bowl rings before he ever played in a regular season NFL game?

a. Pete Banaszak, Raiders
b. Andy Frederick, Cowboys
c. Joe Gilliam, Steelers
d. Cliff Stoudt, Steelers
e. Fran Tarkenton, Vikings
f. Godfrey Zaunbrecher, Vikings

16. Empty End Zone

Which team is the only one not to score a touchdown in a Super Bowl game?

  a. Dallas
  b. Denver
  c. Kansas City
  d. Miami
  e. Minnesota
  f. Oakland

17. Whitewashed

Which team failed to score at all in a Super Bowl game?

  a. Denver
  b. Los Angeles
  c. Minnesota
  d. Oakland
  e. Pittsburgh
  f. None of the above

18. Lost Horizons

Which of these plays represents the biggest loss in Super Bowl competition?

a. Len Dawson sacked for 9 yards by Willie Davis
b. Joe Namath trapped for 36 yards by Billy Ray Smith
c. Bob Griese sacked by Bob Lilly for 29 yards
d. Jim Marshall's 63 yard "wrong way" run
e. Butch Johnson's 9 yard loss after fumbling on a double reverse
f. John Matuszak's 17 yard sack of Ron Jaworski

19. Home Cookin'

Which is the only team to play a Super Bowl in its own stadium?

a. Dallas Cowboys
b. Detroit Lions
c. Los Angeles Rams
d. Miami Dolphins
e. Oakland Raiders
f. None of the above

20. A Day to Remember

January 15, 1978, wasa significant date for Dallas's Randy White. Why?

   a. It was his birthday and he shared Super Bowl co-most valuable player honors with Harvey Martin.

   b. It was the day he moved from middle linebacker to defensive tackle.

   c. It was the day he invented the ''flex'' defense.

   d. It was the day he got married (before Super Bowl XII).

   e. It was the day he turned 21 years old.

   f. It was the day he was drafted by the Cowboys and the U.S. Army.

21. Solitary Man

Who is the only Oakland player to appear in the first three of the Raiders' Super Bowl games (II, XI, and XV)?

   a. Pete Banaszak, running back

   b. Fred Biletnikoff, wide receiver

   c. George Blanda, quarterback-kicker

   d. Jim Otto, center

   e. Gene Upshaw, guard

   f. Warren Wells, wide receiver

22. Everybody Wants to Get Into the Act

On only two occasions has a Super Bowl team had eight different receivers catch passes. Name the two teams

    a. Dallas and Denver
    b. Kansas City and Minnesota
    c. Minnesota and Los Angeles
    d. Oakland and Pittsburgh
    e. Philadelphia and Pittsburgh
    f. Washington and Green Bay

23. Mr. November *and* January

Name the only player in history to quarterback a team in a Rose Bowl, Grey Cup (CFL), and a Super Bowl?

    a. Terry Bradshaw
    b. Len Dawson
    c. Joe Kapp
    d. Warren Moon
    e. Earl Morrall
    f. Fran Tarkenton

24. Perfection

Which two coaches listed below has won every Super Bowl in which his team has played?

a. Bud Grant, Vikings, and Hank Stram, Chiefs
b. Tom Landry, Cowboys, and Bud Grant, Vikings
c. Red Miller, Broncos, and Chuck Noll, Steelers
d. Chuck Noll, Steelers, and Tom Flores, Raiders
e. Don Shula, Colts and Dolphins, and Tom Flores, Raiders
f. Hank Stram, Chiefs, and Don McCafferty, Colts.

25. Straight and True

Which player holds the Super Bowl record for the longest field goal?

a. Don Chandler, Packers
b. Roy Gerela, Steelers
c. Bob Lee, Vikings
d. Jim Turner, Broncos
e. Jan Stenerud, Chiefs
f. Garo Yepremian, Dolphins

26. Pick It Up and Run

Which player holds the Super Bowl record for the longest return of a recovered fumble?

- a. Lance Alworth, Cowboys
- b. Mike Bass, Redskins
- c. Willie Brown, Raiders
- d. Reggie Harrison, Steelers
- e. Randy Hughes, Cowboys
- f. Bobby Walden, Steelers

27. It was in the Cards

Name the only team to win the Super Bowl as a wild card entry.

- a. Atlanta
- b. Kansas City
- c. Los Angeles
- d. Oakland
- e. Miami
- f. No team has ever done it.

28. Super Sites

Name the only city to host the Super Bowl in two different stadiums.

- a. Houston
- b. Los Angeles
- c. Miami
- d. New Orleans
- e. Pontiac
- f. Seattle

29. Do It Again, Again

Three coaches have won back-to-back Super Bowls, but only one accomplished the feat twice. Who is he?

   a. Weeb Ewbank, Jets
   b. Tom Landry, Cowboys
   c. Vince Lombardi, Packers
   d. Chuck Noll, Steelers
   e. Don Shula, Dolphins
   f. Hank Stram, Chiefs

30. Good Field Position

Which player set a Super Bowl record by returning five kickoffs 162 yards for a 25.9-yard average?

   a. Larry Anderson, Steelers
   b. Billy Campfield, Eagles
   c. Jim Duncan, Colts
   d. Mercury Morris, Dolphins
   e. Preston Pearson, Colts
   f. Rick Upchurch, Broncos

31. The One and Only

Who is the only man to play in a Super Bowl and, later, take a team to a Super Bowl as head coach?

  a. Herb Adderley
  b. Forrest Gregg
  c. Joe Kapp
  d. Tom Landry
  e. Vince Lombardi
  f. Chuck Noll

32. Follow the Bouncing Ball

Which two teams combined to *set* the Super Bowl record of 10 turnovers in one game?

  a. Kansas City and Green Bay, Super Bowl I
  b. Baltimore and the New York Jets, Super Bowl III
  c. Kansas City and Minnesota, Super Bowl IV
  d. Baltimore and Dallas, Super Bowl V
  e. Minnesota and Pittsburgh, Super Bowl IX
  f. Dallas and Denver, Super Bowl XII

33. Look Ma, No Hands

Which team set the Super Bowl single-game record for turnovers with eight?

    a. Baltimore, Super Bowl III
    b. Baltimore, Super Bowl V
    c. Denver, Super Bowl XII
    d. Pittsburgh, Super Bowl XIII
    e. Los Angeles, Super Bowl XIV
    f. Oakland, Super Bowl XV

34. Block That Kick

Which four men are *credited* with the only blocked punts in Super Bowl history?

    a. Matt Blair, Ray Guy, Alan Page, and Dick Butkus
    b. Lance Alworth, Alan Page, Joe Greene, and Jack Lambert
    c. Matt Blair, Reggie Harrison, Fred McNeill, and Derrick Jensen
    d. Mitch Hoopes, Ray Guy, Bobby Walden, and Jeff Hayes
    e. Thomas Henderson, Gus Otto, Tom Jackson, and Kellen Winslow
    f. Max McGee, Charles Philyaw, Skip Thomas, and Lester Hayes

35. A Time for Everything

True or False? When Cincinnati and San Francisco met in Super Bowl XVI, it marked the first time since Super Bowl I the game featured two teams new to the game.

36. Breaking the Ice

Which player scored the first points in Super Bowl history?

- a. Willie Davis, Packers
- b. Len Dawson, Chiefs
- c. Max McGee, Packers
- d. Bart Starr, Packers
- e. Jan Stenerud, Chiefs
- f. Jerrel Wilson, Chiefs

37. Getting Ahead

Which two assistant coaches from the Super Bowl II teams—the Green Bay Packers and Oakland Raiders—later became head coaches for their respective teams?

- a. Bill Austin, Packers, and Tom Dahms, Raiders
- b. John (Red) Cochran, Packers, and John Rauch, Raiders
- c. Dave Hanner, Packers, and Don Shinnick, Raiders
- d. John Madden, Raiders, and Phil Bengtson, Packers
- e. Don Shula, Raiders, and Monte Clark, Packers
- f. Bart Starr, Packers, and John Madden, Raiders

38. Share the Wealth

True or False? In Super Bowl III, the Jets' secondary made four interceptions, each of the four defensive backs getting one.

39. Role Reversal

In Super Bowl IV, a Kansas City wide receiver did more damage running the ball than catching passes. Name him.

    a. Chris Burford
    b. Mike Garrett
    c. Frank Pitts
    d. Gloster Richardson
    e. Goldie Sellers
    f. Otis Taylor

40. The Kid's a Real Bearcat

Rookie Jim O'Brien's 32-yard field goal won Super Bowl V for the Baltimore Colts. Which college did he attend?

    a. Alabama
    b. Bethune-Cookman
    c. Cincinnati
    d. Hillsdale
    e. Northwestern
    f. Pepperdine

41. Before America's Team

Prior to winning Super Bowl VI, the Dallas Cowboys often were referred to by what term, supposedly because they "couldn't win the big one?"

    a. The not quite ready for prime time players
    b. Next year's champions
    c. The over the hill gang
    d. The big apples
    e. Monsters of the Midway
    f. The also-rans

42. Understudy

Which Redskins quarterback was Billy Kilmer's backup in Super Bowl VII?

    a. Gary Cuozzo
    b. George Izo
    c. Randy Johnson
    d. Sonny Jurgensen
    e. Harry Theofiledes
    f. Sam Wyche

43. Not a Household Name

Although he seldom started a game, this reserve defensive back was a special teams member, playing in Super Bowl IX with Minnesota and Super Bowl XII with Denver. Name him.

- a. Terry Brown
- b. Steve Craig
- c. Ron Egloff
- d. Randy Poltl
- e. Randy Rich
- f. Godwin Turk

44. Flip-Flop

He no longer plays tight end, but this present day Pittsburgh Steeler caught a key pass in a scoring drive, which was capped by his four-yard touchdown reception, in Super Bowl IX. Who is he?

- a. Larry Anderson
- b. Larry Brown
- c. Frank Lewis
- d. Gerry Mullins
- e. Lynn Swann
- f. Mike Webster

45. Now That I Have Your Attention

Which player returned the opening kickoff 53 yards on a reverse in Super Bowl X?

   a. Larry Anderson, Steelers
   b. Warren Capone, Cowboys
   c. Thomas Henderson, Cowboys
   d. Preston Pearson, Steelers
   e. Preston Pearson, Cowboys
   f. Dave Reavis, Steelers

46. It Came from Outer Space

Which Oakland Raiders defensive end in Super Bowl XI once had his alma mater identified by sportscaster Alex Karras as the "University of Mars"?

   a. Rik Bonness
   b. John Matuszak
   c. Manny Sistrunk
   d. Otis Sistrunk
   e. Dave Rowe
   f. Jack Tatum

47. You Really Know How to Hurt a Guy

Which Denver quarterback lost a Super Bowl to Dallas's Roger Staubach, a man with whom he once contested for the Cowboys' starting position?

a. Eddie LeBaron
b. Clint Longley
c. Don Meredith
d. Craig Morton
e. Dan Reeves
f. Norris Weese

48. I'll Take That

Which reserve Dallas linebacker scored a 37-yard touchdown in Super Bowl XIII after taking the ball out of the grasp of Pittsburgh quarterback Terry Bradshaw?

a. Bob Breunig
b. Guy Brown
c. Mike Hegman
d. Thomas Henderson
e. Bruce Huther
f. D.D. Lewis

49. Drawing the Steel Curtain

The Steelers managed only one interception against the Rams in Super Bowl XIV. Who got it?

   a. Mel Blount, cornerback
   b. Robin Cole, linebacker
   c. Thom Dornbrook, guard
   d. Jack Lambert, linebacker
   e. Donnie Shell, safety
   f. J.T. Thomas, safety

50. Gathering Dust

In Super Bowl XV, Oakland and Philadelphia punters set a new record for the fewest punts. What was their total?

   a. 0
   b. 2
   c. 3
   d. 4
   e. 5
   f. 6

51. Cautious

Prior to Super Bowl XVI, in which both the Bengals' Ken Anderson and the 49ers' Joe Montana each scored touchdowns, only one quarterback had run for a touchdown in a Super Bowl game. Name him.

   a. Len Dawson, Chiefs, Super Bowl IV
   b. Joe Kapp, Vikings, Super Bowl IV
   c. Joe Namath, Jets, Super Bowl III
   d. Roger Staubach, Cowboys, Super Bowl XIII
   e. Fran Tarkenton, Vikings, Super Bowl VIII
   f. Danny White, Cowboys, Super Bowl XII

52. Beginner's Luck

Who was the first rookie defensive back in Super Bowl history to make an interception?

   a. Randy Beverly, cornerback, Jets, Super Bowl III
   b. Mel Blount, cornerback, Steelers, Super Bowl IX
   c. Dwight Hicks, safety, 49ers, Super Bowl XVI
   d. Ronnie Lott, cornerback, 49ers, Super Bowl XVI
   e. Carlton Williamson, safety, 49ers, Super Bowl XVI
   f. Eric Wright, cornerback, 49ers, Super Bowl XVI

53. Only the Scoreboard Counts

Name the only team in Super Bowl history to gain more total yards than its opponent and lose the game.

  a. Chiefs, Super Bowl I
  b. Colts, Super Bowl III
  c. Chiefs, Super Bowl IV
  d. Dallas, Super Bowl X
  e. Broncos, Super Bowl XII
  f. Bengals, Super Bowl XVI

54. High-Mileage Performance

Who was the reserve cornerback who set a record with a 98-yard kickoff return for a touchdown in Super Bowl XVII?

  a. Vernon Dean
  b. William Judson
  c. Lyle Blackwood
  d. Don McNeal
  e. Darrell Green
  f. Fulton Walker

Strength in Reserve

Jim Plunkett has led the Raiders to two Super Bowl victories in the past four seasons (XV and XVIII). In each of those super years he replaced the Raiders' regular quarterback during the season. First it was Dan Pastorini, then it was Marc Wilson.

Answers Super Trivia

1. e. Pontiac, Michigan, was the site of Super Bowl XVI, January 24, 1982.
2. f. Starr was named most valuable player in Super Bowls I and II, and was Green Bay's head coach from 1975–83.
3. c. Holub played linebacker for the Kansas City Chiefs in Super Bowl I and center in Super Bowl IV.
4. c. In Super Bowl V, McCafferty's Colts defeated the Cowboys 16–13.
5. False. The Green Bay Packers (NFL) won Super Bowls I and II, but the New York Jets (AFL) won Super Bowl III and the Kansas City Chiefs (AFL) won Super Bowl IV.
6. True. Herb Adderley, cornerback; Willie Davis, defensive end; Forrest Gregg, tackle; Ray Nitschke, linebacker; Bart Starr, quarterback; and Jim Taylor, fullback.
7. d. Pastorini started the season, but broke his leg in the fifth game. He was replaced by Jim Plunkett.
8. d. Martin, a linebacker, had three interceptions against Philadelphia in Super Bowl XV.
9. e. Allen ran 74 yards in Super Bowl XVIII against the Redskins. He scored on the run.
10. b. Running back King's pass play was good for 80 yards and a touchdown in Super Bowl XV.
11. c. Tight end Ross's 11 receptions for 104 yards in Super Bowl XVI included two touchdown catches.
12. f. They all share the record for rushing touchdowns in one game.
13. b. Chandler in Super Bowl I and Gerela in Super Bowl XIII, and Chris Bahr in Super Bowl XVIII.
14. c. In Super Bowl VIII, Griese attempted seven passes, completed six for 73 yards and no touchdowns.
15. d. Quarterback Stoudt was on the Super Bowl XIII and XIV champion Pittsburgh Steelers, but did not play in a regular season game until 1980, his third season.
16. d. Miami scored only a field goal in Super Bowl VI.
17. f. No team has ever been shut out in a Super Bowl game.
18. c. The loss occurred in Super Bowl VI.
19. f. The Rams, however, came close by playing Super

Bowl XIV at Pasadena's Rose Bowl.

20. a.

21. e.

22. c. In Super Bowl VIII, Fran Tarkenton (18 for 28) threw passes to: Chuck Foreman (5 catches), John Gilliam (4), Stu Voigt, (3), Ed Marinaro (2), Bill Brown (1), Doug Kingsriter (1), Jim Lash (1), and Oscar Reed (1).

In Super Bowl XIV, Vince Ferragamo (15 for 25) spread his passes among: Cullen Bryant, (3), Wendell Tyler (3), Billy Waddy (3), Preston Dennard (2), Terry Nelson (2), Drew Hill (1), and Lawrence McCutcheon (1). McCutcheon also completed a touchdown pass to Ron Smith.

23. c. Kapp quarterbacked the University of California in the 1959 Rose Bowl, the British Columbia Lions in the 1963 and 1964 Grey Cup games, and the Minnesota Vikings in Super Bowl IV. Flores has won Super Bowls XV and XVIII.

24. d. The Steelers under Chuck Noll won Super Bowls IX, X, XIII, and XIV.

25. e. Stenerud kicked a 48-yard field goal in Super Bowl IV. He made all three attempts in the game (25, 32, and 48 yards).

26. b. Bass scored a 49-yard touchdown on Garo Yepremian's ill-fated pass attempt on a blocked Miami field goal play in Super Bowl VII.

27. d. Oakland won Super Bowl XV to become the only wild card team to do so since the wild card concept was initiated in 1970.

28. d. New Orleans hosted Super Bowls IV, VI, and IX at Tulane Stadium and Super Bowls XII and XV at the Lousiana Superdome.
Other Super Bowl sites are:
Tampa Stadium, Tampa, Florida XVIII
Rose Bowl, Pasadena, California . . . . . .XVII, XIV, XI
Pontiac Silverdome, Pontiac, Michigan XVI
Orange Bowl, Miami, Florida. . . . . . .XIII, X, V, III, II

Rice Stadium, Houston, Texas VIII
Memorial Coliseum, Los Angeles, California .... VII, I
29. d. Pittsburgh's Chuck Noll won Super Bowls IX and X, and XIII and XIV. Green Bay's Vince Lombardi won Super Bowls I and II. Miami's Don Shula won Super Bowls VII and VIII.
30. a. In Super Bowl XIV, Anderson's kickoff returns were a major factor in the Steelers' victory.
31. b. Gregg played in Super Bowls I and II with Green Bay and VI with Dallas. He coached Cincinnati in Super Bowl XVI. Tom Flores was a member of the Chiefs' Super Bowl team but did not play in the game.
32. d. The Colts lost three of five fumbles and had three passes intercepted. The Cowboys lost their only fumble and also had three passes intercepted. In Super Bowl XII, Dallas and Denver *tied* the record.
33. c. The Broncos lost four fumbles and four interceptions.
34. c. Blair blocked one of Bobby Walden's punts in Game IX. Harrison blocked one of Mitch Hoopes's punts in Game X. McNeill blocked one of Ray Guy's punts in Game XI. Jensen blocked one of Jeff Hayes's punts in Game XVIII.
35. False. The first two "new" teams met in Super Bowl (not counting Game I) was Super Bowl III between the Baltimore Colts and New York Jets. Since then, until Game XVI, at least one of the teams has had Super Bowl experience.
36. c. Packers wide receiver Max McGee scored on a 37-yard pass from Bart Starr in Super Bowl I.
37. d. Phil Bengtson was head coach of the Packers from 1968 to 1970; John Madden was the Raiders' head coach from 1969 to 1978.
38. False. Cornerback Randy Beverly had two. Cornerback Johnny Sample had one, and safety Jim Hudson had one. Safety Bill Baird had none.
39. c. Pitts caught three passes for 33 yards, but in three critical situations he ran reverses and gained a total of 37

yards.

40. c.

41. b.

42. f. Sonny Jurgensen injured his foot during the regular season, leaving Sam Wyche as the only other active quarterback on Washington's roster for the game.

43. d.

44. b. Larry Brown is presently an offensive tackle.

45. c. Henderson circled back, took a handoff from Preston Pearson, and returned the ball 53 yards to the Pittsburgh 44-yard line

46. d. Sistrunk actually did not attend college, but his great size, fierce play, and clean-shaven head helped prompt the mythical alma mater.

47. d. Morton and Staubach were rivals for the Dallas quarterback job from 1969 to 1974. They played against each other in Super Bowl XII.

48. c.

49. d. Lambert's interception stopped a late Rams' drive and clinched the Steelers' fourth Super Bowl victory.

50. f. The Raiders' Ray Guy punted three times for a 42.0-yard average; the Eagles' Max Runager punted three times for an average of 36.7.

51. e. The Vikings' only score in the 24–7 loss to the Dolphins was Tarkenton's four-yard run in the fourth quarter.

52. f.

53. f. The Bengals gained 356 yards to the 49ers 275, but San Francisco won 26–21.

54. f.

ABOUT THE AUTHORS

Ted Brock, 41, was born in Los Angeles and grew up in the San Francisco Bay area, where his appreciation of football was enriched by an incurable sentimentality about the University of California Bears and the San Francisco 49ers. Before joining NFL Properties, Inc. as an associate editor in 1977, he worked as a high school English teacher and a freelance sports writer.

Jim Campbell, 47, is a native of Pennsylvania. He and Brock have co-authored "NFL Trivia" for *PRO!*, the official magazine of the NFL, for three seasons. A graduate of Susquehanna University, Campbell has been on the staff of NFL Properties, Inc. since 1977. Prior to that he was an historian at the Pro Football Hall of Fame in Canton, Ohio.